£2.60

The Paradox of the Liar

Contributors

Alan R. Anderson
University of Pittsburgh

Keith S. Donnellan
Cornell University

Frederic B. Fitch
Yale University

Bas C. van Fraassen
University of Toronto

Newton Garver
State University of New York at Buffalo

Hans Herzberger
University of Toronto

John Kearns
State University of New York at Buffalo

Robert L. Martin
Livingston College, Rutgers University

John L. Pollock
State University of New York at Buffalo

Brian Skyrms
University of Illinois at Chicago Circle

The Paradox of the Liar

edited by Robert L. Martin

Yale University Press, 1970
New Haven and London

Library of Congress catalog card number: 79-118732

International standard book number: 0-300-01355-8

Designed by Sally Sullivan,

set in IBM Documentary type,

and printed in the United States of America by The Carl Purington Rollins Printing Office of the Yale University Press.

Distributed in Great Britain, Europe, and Africa by Yale University Press, Ltd., London; in Canada by McGill-Queen's University Press, Montreal; in Mexico by Centro Interamericano de Libros Académicos, Mexico City; in Australasia by Australia and New Zealand Book Co., Pty., Ltd., Artarmon, New South Wales; in India by UBS Publishers' Distributors Pvt., Ltd., Delhi; in Japan by John Weatherhill, Inc., Tokyo.

Contents

Preface

The essays collected here, all published for the first time, are revised versions of papers presented at a Symposium-Workshop entitled "Recent Work on the Liar Paradox." The meetings were held in Buffalo, New York, in March 1969, under the sponsorship of the Program in Logic and Philosophy of Science of the Department of Philosophy, State University of New York at Buffalo. Although the format of the symposium called for the presentation of three solutions to the Liar, the actual yield was more than twice that number. In many cases commentators closed their remarks with "suggestions" or "modest proposals." These provoked further discussion in which positions were contrasted and modified; much of the discussion has found its way into these papers.

I wish to thank the participants in the symposium for their enthusiastic cooperation in the project from its inception to its culmination in this volume. I also wish to thank the members of the Philosophy Department of the State University of New York at Buffalo, and especially William T. Parry, Chairman, for generous support of the symposium and help in its planning. Financial assistance from Livingston College of Rutgers University made possible the early completion of my part of the editorial work on the volume. The bibliography is mainly the work of Mr. Richard J. Wallace.

R. L. M.

The word 'presupposition' has several different senses in ordinary usage, but there is a technical sense of the term which lies at the heart of Bas van Fraassen's solution to the Liar. In this sense, if a sentence $\underline{A}$ presupposes a sentence $\underline{B}$, then unless $\underline{B}$ is true $\underline{A}$ is neither true nor false. 'Presupposition' has been given this sense explicitly by Strawson in connection with his discussion of referring: 'All John's children are asleep' is said to presuppose 'John has children', so that the truth of the latter is required for the truth or falsity of the former. Van Fraassen calls upon this notion of presupposition to explain the fact that the Liar sentence has no truth-value, though in the case of the Liar it is not an existential presupposition that fails.

Naturally this approach requires the acceptance of a language which is not bivalent — a language in which there are sentences that are neither true nor false. In this connection van Fraassen employs a technique that he developed earlier, involving the notion of supervaluation, which allows the inclusion of truth-value-less sentences in formal languages in a way which, remarkably enough, does no violence to the set of truths of classical two-valued logic. For example, a sentence '$\underline{p}$ v ~$\underline{p}$' is true under every interpretation of the language, even in cases where, for reasons of failure of presupposition, the sentence '$\underline{p}$' is neither true nor false. The supervaluation technique, incidentally, is adopted by both Skyrms and Martin in their papers. It is discussed critically by Hans Herzberger in his commentary on van Fraassen's paper.

To examine the theoretical structure in which van Fraassen's solution to the Liar is imbedded, Herzberger compares an alternative system in his commentary. He too is interested in formal languages in which sentences may be neither true nor false, and he accepts a notion of presupposition quite in accord with van Fraassen's discussion. But he introduces an additional theoretical notion, the security of a sentence, based on an insight of the medieval philosopher, Jean Buridan. Buridan's idea, in modern dress, is that correspondence conditions for a sentence (that the case is as the sentence signifies) can be satisfied independently of the presuppositions.

A sentence such as 'The present king of France is a king' has an element of veracity to it, so the argument goes, despite the failure of its presupposition, and Herzberger calls this element of veracity the security of the sentence: "security" becomes his term for "correspondence with reality," and is regarded as a constituent of truth but not all of it.

Herzberger's alternative to the supervaluation approach is a three-valued treatment of the connectives proposed in 1938 by D. A. Bochvar. However Bochvar's system lacks an advantage of the supervaluation approach: very special rules of inference are needed in Bochvar's system because the set of valid sentences (still classically conceived as the set of sentences true under every interpretation) is not the same as the set of valid sentences for classical bivalent systems. At this point Herzberger reintroduces Buridan, suggesting as a revised notion of validity the property of security under all interpretations—valid sentences are those sentences that are not false under any interpretation (though they may also be nontrue). The resultant system, which Herzberger calls "BB" (Buridan-Bochvar) is presented in detail in an appendix to the paper.

John F. Kearns treats two main topics in his commentary: presupposition and vagueness. Kearns first remarks that on Frege's view a sentence retains sense (expresses a proposition) even if it has an existential presupposition that fails. What the sentence 'The present king of France is bald' loses when its existential presupposition (in this case 'There is a present king of France') fails, is its truth value. Frege's view here depends on his conception of the True and the False (see the discussion of Frege in Anderson's introduction), which Kearns is prepared to reject. The upshot for Kearns is that one may dispense with the notion that failure of presupposition (at least presupposition of the Fregean sort) causes "truth-value gaps"—sentences that are neither true nor false. Kearns suggests that if an existential presupposition is false, the sentence which presupposes it may also be regarded as false, though false for a different reason. Kearns then suggests that van Fraassen has actually followed Strawson in dealing with a more general notion of presupposition in which the truth of the presupposition seems to be required for the significance (or sense) of a sentence. Kearns has something in mind here similar to the category notion explored in the papers by Martin, Donnellan, and Garver: to say that something is green presupposes for significance that it is a physical object. But Kearns argues that it is not fruitful to look upon the Liar as involving the failure of a presupposition of this kind, and he turns to an alternative proposal based on the notion of vagueness.

A predicate is considered vague, in Kearns' sense, if it has borderline cases. If some individual a is a borderline case for a predicate 'R' then Kearns suggests that both 'R(a)' and its negation, '~R(a)' are neither true nor false. Building on this general notion, he sees the Liar as showing that our concepts of truth and falsity are not only vague, but incorrigibly so. He discusses the introduction of "new" truth-predicates expressing "stronger" concepts of truth than those whose incorrigible vagueness has been demonstrated, and suggests that the Liarlike difficulties encountered at each new level show that our conceptual framework is "essentially open-ended."

In his rejoinder to Herzberger and Kearns, van Fraassen notes that for the most part his critics have been concerned with his conception of the structure of language, rather than with the details of his analysis. After some brief remarks on Kearns' notion of vagueness (van Fraassen suggests a "presuppositional analysis" of vagueness) he turns to the more general matters. He suggests and develops an analogy between the role of the semantic paradoxes in the philosophy of language and the role of the Antinomies in the development of Kant's philosophy of the physical world. What emerges is a defense of the use of supervaluations, presented as a prelude to a consideration of some of the specific misgivings expressed by Herzberger. Van Fraassen calls attention to an interesting point of dispute. We have spoken, in connection with van Fraassen's system, of sentences with no truth-value, and we have also noted that Herzberger compares van Fraassen's system to systems of three-valued logic. Van Fraassen argues in his rejoinder that it is a mistake to view sentences which are neither true nor false in his system as having some third truth-value. He suggests that this mistake is responsible for the view (which he also regards as mistaken) that the logical connective '≡' in his system does not express material equivalence. Van Fraassen ends his rejoinder with remarks on the equivalence of the supervaluation technique with certain matrix treatments.

The solution proposed by Brian Skyrms is based on weakening the classical principle of substitutivity with respect to identity. The principle states that a truth containing some name or referring expression 'a' remains a truth when 'a' is replaced by a name or referring expression 'b', so long as a and b are identical—the truth-value of a sentence about some object is not affected by changes in the way the object is named or referred to. There are certain kinds of linguistic contexts in which problems arise for this principle of substitutivity—to use the well-known example, it is true that George IV wished to know whether Scott was the author of Waverly, and it is true that Scott and the author of Waverly were identical, yet it is surely not true that George IV wished to know whether Scott was Scott. The cluster of questions concerning restrictions on substitutivity with respect to identity in such epistemic contexts (and also in modal contexts) has been the subject of much debate in the philosophical literature, but Skyrms appears to be the first to raise the question in connection with semantical self-reference. The Liar, he suggests, teaches us that situations of the following kind may arise: A sentence whose name we form with single quotation marks in the usual way, and which also has assigned to it the name '$\underline{a}$', is neither true nor false. In particular it is not true, and we may assert this fact by affixing the predicate '~T' ('is not true') to the quotation-name of the sentence. But now, despite the fact that the quotation-name and the letter '$\underline{a}$' are both names of this one nontrue sentence, if we replace the quotation-name by the letter '$\underline{a}$' in the true assertion of nontruth described above, the resultant sentence is without truth-value. Of course the sentence for which this distressing result obtains is the Strengthened Liar, '~T$\underline{a}$'. Skyrms argues that the trouble lies in our using the principle of substitutivity, "which was developed to handle bivalent sentences," in connection with sentences that are without truth-value. It is clear that substitution leads us in cases like the one above into semantical self-reference, and Skyrms shows that by restricting substitutivity to sentences which are true or false we disarm the Strengthened Liar.

Much of Skyrms' paper is concerned with the problem of extending his formal language through the introduction of first-order quantification (i.e. with variables ranging over individuals), and he acknowledges that his results here are incomplete. His first step is to allow into the domain of quantification the sentences of the propositional language discussed in his earlier paper on the Liar. Even at this point he is able to show that a restriction on the rule of universal specification is required; this restriction (allowing universal specification only when there is an additional premise to the effect that the sentence specified to is either true or false) allows Skyrms to retain the theory of identity in its unrestricted form, even when quantificational sentences themselves are allowed into the domain. Skyrms concludes by producing a quantificational version of the Strengthened Liar and considers alternative ways of dealing with it.

Frederic Fitch objects to the central idea of Skyrms' solution —the sacrifice of substitutivity with respect to identity. He argues that the situation Skyrms describes, in which a sentence is true of $\underline{a}$ but only neuter of $\underline{b}$, is enough to show, contrary to hypothesis, that $\underline{a}$ and $\underline{b}$ are not identical.

In addition Fitch proposes a solution to the Liar which he claims has the advantage of requiring no modification of classical two-valued logic. Fitch formulates his proposal, as did Kearns, in terms of propositions — not sentences — as the bearers of truth and falsity. Suppose that '$\underline{P}$' is a predicate referring to a property of propositions and '$\underline{s}$' is a well-formed sentence, or name of a proposition (here I follow Fitch's terminology). Then it is not in general the case, Fitch argues, that '$\underline{P}(\underline{s})$', the result of applying '$\underline{P}$' to '$\underline{s}$', is a well-formed sentence. If '$\underline{P}(\underline{s})$' is well-formed it is thought of as a sentence to the effect that the proposition referred to by '$\underline{s}$' has the property referred to by '$\underline{P}$'. However, Fitch specifies conditions that must be met before he would regard '$\underline{P}(\underline{s})$' as well-formed (and thus as capable of expressing a proposition). And indeed the conditions that Fitch specifies are not met in the case of the Liar. Since on his view the Liar sentence is not well-formed, no truth-value gaps are encountered. Sentences are, on Fitch's view, never true or false, and in the case of the Liar sentence no proposition at all is expressed.

John L. Pollock begins his commentary on Skyrms' paper with a statement of what he regards as necessary for producing a solution to the Liar. Arguing that a formal investigation which blocks the derivation of the Liar does not by itself constitute a solution, he requires explanation of the meaning of 'true', and a demonstration that, given that meaning of 'true', the Liar sentence is not paradoxical. Pollock then asks whether there is a reasonable analysis of 'true' that leads to the formal restrictions proposed by Skyrms, and raises a number of questions concerning the failure of unrestricted substitutivity in truth-contexts in Skyrms' system.

Pollock's own proposal for solving the Liar is based on a distinction between the predicate and the operator use of 'true'. Examples of the former are: 'What he said is true', 'The next sentence is true'. An example of the operator use is: 'It is true that it is going to rain'. In the predicate use one must name or somehow refer to what is said to be true; with the operator, one begins with a sentence, not the name of a sentence, and produces a new sentence by affixing the operator, 'it is true that'. Pollock suggests that we take the operator use of 'true' as basic and regard the predicate use as "logically derived" from the operator use, because no paradoxes can be generated if we use 'true' only as an operator. Then he examines ways in which the predicate use can be defined in terms of the operator use, and suggests a general requirement that must be met not only in the case of 'true' but for any predicate that is defined in terms of an operator. This requirement guards against paradox and still allows a definition of the predicate use of 'true' that is said to capture its meaning in English.

Robert L. Martin agrees with van Fraassen and Skyrms that the Liar and the Strengthened Liar are well-formed but lacking

in truth-value. Along with van Fraassen, he takes it that a presupposition of a sentence of the form F̲a is that some criterion of
application of the predicate F̲ be satisfied by the term a̲. Thus a
sentence such as "The number two is green" is without truth-value
because its presupposition — the number two falls within the range
of applicability of the predicate 'is green' — is false. The Liar is
clearly not a category-mistake on a par with such sentences as
'Two is green' and 'Virtue is triangular', but a satisfactory test of
semantical correctness (i.e. freedom from category-incorrectness),
when applied to the paradoxical sentences, will never yield the result that these sentences have passed the test, though it does pass
other self-referential sentences and even some self-referential
sentences with semantical predicates.

In the second part a formal language is presented. It is capable of self-reference and has built into it the machinery of the category solution. Predicates are assigned not only extensions but
also RA's — ranges of applicability — under interpretations. Appendix A contains a proof that an interpretation may be devised under
which the language expresses its own truth concept, as long as the
predicate whose extension is the set of sentences true under that
interpretation is restricted in its RA to the set of sentences which
are true or false under the interpretation.

The Strengthened Liar presents special problems for this solution, and Keith S. Donnellan's commentary contains two criticisms.
Whereas the "plain" Liar is generally taken to be the self-referential assertion 'This very sentence is false', the Strengthened Liar
asserts, a bit more coyly, 'This very sentence is not true', or a bit
less coyly, 'This very sentence is either false or without truth-value'.
The extra trouble caused by the Strengthened Liar can be seen as
follows. Suppose we have disarmed the sentence by showing in some
way that it is neither true nor false. But then it is not true (and not
false), which is just what the Strengthened Liar is taken to assert.
Hence, apparently, it is true.

Donnellan first shows that a restriction on the range of applicability of disjunctive predicates, which was introduced in an earlier
paper to cope with the Strengthened Liar, was not incorporated into
the formal language. Donnellan shows that its absence allows an un-
welcome reappearance of the Strengthened Liar. There are ways of
correcting the situation, and Donnellan suggests one way, but then
he turns to what seems to him a more fundamental objection. This
has to do primarily with restricting the range of applicability of the
predicates 'is true' and 'is false' to the set of sentences which are
true or false; it also involves a distinction made in several papers
between "choice" and "exclusion" negation (Herzberger calls the
first "negation" and the second "complementation"). The distinction
is relevant only to languages which are not bivalent. The choice

negation of a sentence is true if and only if the sentence negated is false; the exclusion negation is true if and only if the sentence negated is either false or without truth-value. Intuitively, exclusion negation just guarantees that truth is excluded; choice negation tells us that the other truth-value characterizes the sentence negated. The category approach seems to require that we give up exclusion negation, but Donnellan objects that it is the loss, not of exclusion negation, but of the applicability of 'is true' and 'is false' to truth-valueless sentences that creates serious problems for Martin's approach. For once we see that the Liar sentence, for example, is without truth-value, then it seems clear that it is not true, and the 'not' here can be choice negation as long as we allow that the assertion that the Liar is true is simply false.

Newton Garver raises the question of whether there are not further conditions, beyond category-correctness, which must be satisfied before a sentence can be said to be true or false. He suggests that besides grammatical, definitional, referential, and categorial criteria of meaning there are also what he calls "situational" criteria. In this connection Garver endorses the idea that propositions or statements — in any case not sentences — are true or false. Garver's notion of "situational" meaning plays a crucial role once the proposition–sentence distinction is made, since features of the situation will have an effect on what proposition, if any, is expressed by an utterance of a sentence. Garver argues that talking of propositions or statements as true or false would provide a way out of Donnellan's second objection to this solution. He suggests more generally that further progress against the Liar will depend on explicit attention to the situational complexities that surround the production of speech-acts.

The reply to Donnellan and Garver has three parts. First the technical mistake pointed out by Donnellan is corrected. Then it is argued that an answer to his more general objection is already contained in the approach as it has been developed so far, though not in the formal treatment. Finally Martin claims that the proposition–sentence distinction does not provide a way around Donnellan's objection, and that a formulation of the Liar in terms of propositions or statements raises many of the same issues concerning sentences, that occupy those who deal with the Liar solely in terms of sentences.

St. Paul's Epistle to Titus

by Alan Ross Anderson

The papers to follow this introduction are devoted to technical studies of a logical problem raised in antiquity. My task, as I understand it, is to say something which might help one see why the antique problem is still with us, and why it seems to require modern dress. The contemporary clothing consists in large part of notions and notation from the very recent past, barely more than 100 years old. But the problem has some interesting historical features, on which I will dwell briefly before bringing us up to date.

I

We learn from the scriptures that St. Paul had, on the isle of Crete, a bishop named Titus, who had been sent there to minister to the spiritual needs of the faithful and spread the gospel among the heathen. The latter must have been a rather difficult task, in view of certain moral shortcomings on the part of the inhabitants of Crete. In verses 12-13 of Chapter 1 of his Epistle, St. Paul writes severely to Titus as follows:

εἰπέν τις ἐξ αὐτῶν ἴδιος αὐτῶν προφήτης
Κρῆτες ἀεὶ ψεῦσται, κακὰ θηρία, γαστέρες
ἀργαί. ἡ μαρτυρία αὕτη ἐστὶν ἀληθής.

The strength of the biblical tradition can be illustrated by a number of translations. Thus the Vulgate:

Dixit quidam ex illis proprius ipsorum propheta: 'Cretenses semper mendaces, malae bestiae, ventres pigri.' Testimonium hoc verum est.

King James version:

One of themselves, even a prophet of their own, said, The Cretans are always liars, evil beasts, slow bellies. This witness is true.

1

Douay version:

> One of them a prophet of their own, said, The Cretans are always liars, evil beasts, slothful bellies. This testimony is true.

And the Revised Standard:

> One of themselves, a prophet of their own, said, "Cretans are always liars, evil beasts, lazy gluttons." This testimony is true.

But testimony to the wickedness of the Cretans is not limited to biblical authorities. Henry Alford, Dean of Canterbury at the time of the American Civil War, cites (in his edition of the Greek Testament)[1] an impressive array of ancient writers who tend to support St. Paul's view of the Cretans: they were avaricious (Livy, Plutarch, Polybius), ferocious and fraudulent (Polybius, Strabo, Leonides), and above all liars (Polybius again, but also Diogenianus, Psellus, and Suidas).

It is hard to fly in the face of evidence like this, though one wishes, in the interest of justice, that there were extant some defense against these charges. The historical case seems, as it stands, to be one-sided.[2]

Somehow the statement that Cretans always lie got to be attributed to one Epimenides, a citizen of Phaestus (according to Diogenes Laertius, writing nearly one thousand years after the fact), and a native of Cnossus, the capital city of the island. None of the writings of Epimenides survive, but some sense of the historical accuracy of the attribution can be gained from the following sentences attributed to Diogenes Laertius. He says, concerning Epimenides:

> One day he was sent into the country by his father to look for a stray sheep, and at noon he turned aside out of the way, and went to sleep in a cave, where he slept for fifty-seven years. [I.109]

---

1. Henry Alford, D.D., ed., The Greek Testament (3d ed., 4 vols., London and Cambridge, 1862). This extraordinarily comprehensive and learned treatment is a source of much information about the infamy of Cretans.

2. One is reminded of a monologue of Mark Twain's about Satan (whom he understood to be one of his own ancestors). He pointed out that no one had heard much of Satan's side of the case (against which so much noise had been made by anti-Satanists), and that this seemed unfair, adding: "To my mind, this procedure is irregular. It is un-American. It is un-English. It is French."

What we learn from such anecdotes is, I suppose, that our forebears were a little more credulous than we are, at least as regards historical detail. Whether the credit (or blame) for the puzzle is to be given to Epimenides is moot; in the absence of better evidence we bow to St. Paul, and to a long tradition according to which "the Liar paradox" and "the Epimenides paradox" meant the same thing.

The ancients noted that there was something odd about having a Cretan say (presumably of himself as well as his compatriots) that Cretans always lie, but no one took the problem thus stated seriously, because of the obviousness of the solution. We may suppose, without undue generosity, that at least _once_, at least _one_ Cretan told the truth, even if only by accident, in an unguarded moment (there were lots of Cretans, and we may fairly judge their ineptitude by our own); in which case the statement of Epimenides is simply false: it is just _not_ _true_ that Cretans always lie, and there is an end to the matter. So "the prophet among them" uttered a falsehood, a hazard common among prophets.

But once the hare is loose, the ancients can scamper after it as well as we, and we are (apparently) indebted to Eubulides[3] for sharpening the problem a little. It is after all simply an accident of history that there were so many Cretans. There might, for all we know, have been only one; let him be Epimenides. And in order to fix ideas, let him utter but one sentence: Κρῆτες ἀεὶ ψεῦσται. And now things become a bit stickier. For if what he said was true, then the only Cretan utterance — to wit, his — is false; so if what he said was correct, then it was also wrong.

On the other hand, suppose he spoke falsely in saying that Cretans always lie. Then some Cretan must have spoken truly. But the statement of Epimenides is, by hypothesis, the only example of a Cretan statement; hence it must be true after all.

Rather than draw false inferences about the etymology of the word "cretin" (which has nothing to do with Cretans; it came into English in about 1800, through Swiss patois, surprisingly, from the Latin Christianum, thereby establishing once again connections between our topic and the New Testament), we will try to sharpen the problem a little more and bring out two of its essential features.

3. See Benson Mates, Stoic Logic (Berkeley, University of California Press, 1961), and references there given, and A. N. Prior, "On a Family of Paradoxes," Notre Dame Journal of Formal Logic, 2 (1961), 16–32. The attributions again seem to have dubious merit.

II

The first of these has to do with the notions of truth and falsehood. We can make the role played by these notions a little more picturesque by considering a couple of boxes:

	The sentence in box A is true.
A	B

With an empty box A, this all looks innocuous enough. We can imagine lots of sentences ("Snow is white," "Hollywood is in California," "7 + 5 = 12,"—all true) which, when plugged into box A, would yield a truth in box A, and with it a truth in box B.

We are equally able to imagine sentences for box A ("Snow is black," "Hollywood is in Utah," "7 + 5 = 13") which will produce a falsehood in box A, and with it a falsehood in box B. And if we look at boxes C and D:

	The sentence in box C is false.
C	D

we can again think of examples. Putting "7 + 5 = 12" in box C gives us a truth there, all right, but gives us a falsehood in D. Whereas putting "7 + 5 = 13" in C gives us a falsehood there, but a truth in D. This should make it clear where the argument is going; we need only consider boxes E and F:

The sentence in box F is true.	The sentence in box E is false.
E	F

Or more simplemindedly:

The sentence in box G is false.
G

Two points emerge from all of this.
  1. The notions of truth and falsity are essential to the odd argument.

2. There is an odd feature, evident indirectly from boxes E and F, and collapsed in box G, having to do with <u>self-reference</u>. We take up these topics one by one.

III

Questions about truth have been asked in a variety of tones of voice for a long time. The fierce question is the one uttered in a deeply anxious tone of voice: "<u>WHAT IS TRUTH</u>?" What is indicated by this question is that the asker is (probably legitimately) worried about something, but not willing to think hard enough about his worries to come up with something answerable. With such "existential" questions we shall not try to deal here, not because they are not interesting, but because they have little interest for liars—our topic.

Toward the end of the nineteenth century a theory was developed by Gottlob Frege (1848–1925) that was designed to answer a simpler, somewhat crisper question about <u>truth</u>. Though Frege would not have put the matter this way, what he said amounts to this. We consider the fact that we talk with each other (about lots of topics, mathematics and logic among them), and that sometimes what we say is true, and sometimes false. Most of us like to speak truly as often as possible (given the constraints of etiquette), but we sometimes speak falsely by mistake, or by design.

What becomes clear from these considerations immediately is that, if we confine ourselves to one small set of crisp questions about truth ("Is what <u>he</u> said <u>true</u>?"), <u>truth</u> and <u>falsity</u> come out to be attached to <u>utterances</u> (sayings, statements, propositions, sentences—something, no matter how it is described, having to do with how we speak to each other).

Given these constraints, that what we <u>say</u> is true or false, at least two theories of the topic are available. Historically, the first of the hardheaded mathematical theories is that of Frege, to the effect that sentences are <u>names</u>—names of an odd sort, admittedly, but names nonetheless. All names, according to his view, had two sorts of significance: their <u>Sinn</u> (or "sense") and their <u>Bedeutung</u> (or "denotation").

At this point we consider an example, and again we yield to a tradition, according to which we are required to make an example of a certain nineteenth-century novelist and poet.

"Scott" <u>denotes</u> Sir Walter Scott.

(I suppose there is some point in keeping these traditions: once one mentions the novelist's name, those familiar with the tradition know what the discussion is about, though of course any other novelist would have done as well. But one might be ruled out of order in such a discussion if the name of Defoe were mentioned, as one would <u>surely</u> be in talking about "the perceptual patch" if one thought it was <u>green</u>. Hume thought it was purple, but in the twentieth century we know better; it is red.)

"The author of Waverly"

also denotes the same person, but, so to speak, under a different guise, or in a different way. That is to say, "Scott" and "the author of Waverly" have the same denotation (to wit, a certain Scottish novelist of the nineteenth century), but the two expressions name the same chap in ways that are at least different enough to make the question

Was Scott the author of Waverly?

make sense. (In asking such a question, we are surely not asking whether Scott was Scott.)

Upshot: "Scott" and "the author of Waverly" have the same denotation (Scott), but different senses. And if we also treat sentences as names, as Frege did, then we can see that sentences like "Napoleon was born in Corsica" and "7 + 5 = 12," though both strikingly different in meaning or content, are notably similar in one respect. "The most striking thing that they do have in common is that both are true."[4] Why not then say simply that they both <u>name</u> (or <u>denote</u>) <u>truth</u>, while doing it in admittedly different ways, just as "Scott" and "the author of Waverly" both denote the same fellow, but in different ways? (There are lots of ways of <u>denoting</u> this man, e.g. "That Scotsman born in 1771 whose favorite book as a child was written by Thomas Percy, and whose first literary works were translations of Bürger and Goethe.")

Compelling reasons for thinking that sentences with different senses may denote the same thing (i.e. truth or falsity) were set forth by Frege, and they have been given their clearest contemporary expression by Alonzo Church. The ideas so put forth are to the writer's mind not only compelling, but beautiful. But every coin has two sides, and it is not surprising that equally eloquent arguments have been brought forth by other writers, among whom we mention Tarski[5] and Quine.

---

4. Alonzo Church, <u>Introduction to Mathematical Logic</u> (Princeton, Princeton University Press, 1956), p. 25.

5. Tarski's original paper has appeared in several languages; for an English version see A. Tarski, <u>Logic</u>, <u>Semantics</u>, <u>Metamathematics</u> (Oxford, Oxford University Press, 1956).

Some of the philosphical bite is provided by Quine,[6] who notes justly that neither Frege nor Church has completed the formal details of a decent mathematical theory of the Sinn of sentences. Of course neither has pretended to;[7] the claim is that "the true story must go something like this . . . ," and in the absence of a proper way of filling out the triple dots, one can appreciate the skepticism of Quine and Goodman, who at one point claimed that the project was hopeless.[8]

Their polemic against Frege's idea that sentences had two pieces: (i) what they expressed (the Sinn), and (ii) the truth or falsity (their Bedeutung) was supported by a theory of truth different from that of Frege, developed by Tarski, and independently by Carnap[9] at about the same time. The account of the matter I shall give has more theoretical than historical accuracy (if it has any at all). In retrospect anyway it can easily look like this.

In the absence of a mathematical theory of truth designed to deal with senses of names ((i) above), the presence of a first-rate theory about denotations (ii) made it look plausible to say that (i) was a fatuously hopeless problem. So we ought, as this theory contends, to concentrate on (ii) alone.

According to this view, truth is not something named by sentences, but is rather a property which some sentences have, and others don't. This still lets us make sense of questions like "Is what he said true?" Truth still has an appropriate connection with people talking to each other, but now we seem to have gotten rid of those ghostly entities called "propositions," or "senses," or Sinne, in favor of simple truth-values.

So according to the Tarskian view, truth is a property possessed by certain strings of symbols in a language, rather than a "thing" denoted by, the sentences which we think of as good. And we notice as a first moral that on either account we are in trouble with sentences like those in box G above. Indeed the Tarskian

---

6. This theme has been recurrent throughout Quine's extensive writings. It is probably best represented in W. V. O. Quine, From a Logical Point of View (Cambridge, Mass., Harvard University Press, 1953), passim. For a searching criticism, see R. L. Cartwright, "Ontology and the Theory of Meaning," Philosophy of Science, 21 (1959), 316–25.

7. Church, p. 67, writes, "We have not, however, attempted to formalize this semantical discussion, or even to put the material into such preliminary order as would constitute a first step toward formalization."

8. Nelson Goodman and W. V. O. Quine, "Steps Toward a Constructive Nominalism," Journal of Symbolic Logic, 12 (1947), 105–22.

9. For historical details, see Tarski, pp. 277–78.

view of truth, which pays attention only to half of Frege's theory, is sufficient to prove one of the simplest and deepest theorems in mathematical logic. It is known as "Tarski's theorem," and a proof is given in Robert Martin's paper in this volume.

All of this brings us to the following point. Given the problem originally attributed to Epimenides, and a sharpening thereof as attributed to Eubulides, we find ourselves in Box G, with two distinct theories of true sentences (or assertions, or statements, or propositions), neither of which helps much. No one much likes to be in Box G, so we turn to the second of the two topics mentioned at the end of II above.

IV

Why don't we say that one or the other of the two recent classical theories of truth as applied to what we say are fine, and that self-reference is at the heart of the difficulty; that if we could simply rule that out we would be in good shape? The difficulty with such a stance is that some of the most profound arguments in logic involve self-reference (in some sense that needs to be made precise).

We first point out that not all self-reference needs to lead to trouble. We look for example at boxes E' and F':

The sentence in box F' is true.

E'

The sentence in box E' is true.

F'

or more simply at

The sentence in box G' is true.

G'

No difficulty seems to ensue here, nor does from invoking "Matthew Arnold's desperate principle that what I say three times is true."[10] So we begin to look at cases like E', F', and G' which seem harmless, and also at arguments which are perilously close to E, F, and G.

---

10. I am sure that I owe this felicitous phrase to Brand Blanshard, but an assiduous search of his writings failed to reveal the source.

I think it is fair to say that one of the principal focal points of twentieth-century studies (thus far, anyway) in the philosophical foundations of mathematics and logic has been to get as close as possible to E, F, and G, without getting close enough to be sunk by inconsistency.

V

At this point it is advisable to look at another example, which, while not so venerable as those of Epimenides and St. Paul, has a respectable history dating from sometime in the nineteenth century. It is difficult, here as in other cases, to pin down the exact historical antecedents; arguments of the sort I shall describe in a moment were "in the air" in nineteenth-century mathematics and have had applications in set theory (Cantor), logic (Russell), recursive function theory (Gödel), and elsewhere. These arguments have a recognizable "family resemblance," but I shall not try to characterize them generally. One example will suffice.

Consider a batch of functions of one argument, defined on the natural numbers, taking natural numbers as values. As instances we may think of that function f which when applied to a number yields its successor; or that function g which when applied to a number yields the triple of the argument; or that function h which when applied to a number first doubles it, then multiplies the result by the largest prime number less than 100, and then divides that result by two. That is to say (for these simple examples),

$$f(x) = x + 1,$$
$$g(x) = 3x, \text{ and}$$
$$h(x) = \frac{2x \cdot 97}{2}$$

Let this batch of functions be denumerably infinite, so that we can match them up with the natural numbers, and then consider the sequence

$$f_0, f_1, f_2, \ldots, f_i, \ldots$$

of such functions, each of which has a subscript indicating its mate among the natural numbers. Nothing in the argument to follow depends on the particular character of the functions involved; all we need to know is that for each i and j, if we apply the i-th function to the natural number j, we get some natural number (say k) as the value of the i-th function when applied to j. That is,

$$f_i(j) = k.$$

What we now show, using a _good_ self-referential argument, is that we can define a function which is _not_ among the _f_'s we have enumerated. For let

$$g(i) = \underline{f}_i(i) + 1.$$

Then let us suppose that _g_ is among the enumerated _f_'s: say it is the _k_-th one, $\underline{f}_k$. None of us needs to know what this function gives when applied t̄ō the argument _k_; we only assume that _g_ (the _k_-th function $\underline{f}_k$) turns out on computation to give us a unique value. Since _g_ is̄ $\underline{f}_k$, we would have

$$g(\underline{k}) = \underline{f}_k(\underline{k}) = \underline{f}_k(\underline{k}) + 1.$$

And this is of course awkward for $\underline{f}_k$ (otherwise known as _g_). We don't of course know _which_ f_k is supposed to do the work assigned to _g_; the point of the argument is that _none_ of them will do it. And if this claim is challenged by, say, the suggestion that "the eighty-third function $\underline{f}_{83}$ will do the work _g_ is supposed to do," the challenge can be met by pointing out that

$$g(83) = \underline{f}_{83}(83) = \underline{f}_{83}(83) + 1.$$

And no matter _what_ number the eighty-third function yields when applied to 83, that number certainly is not the same as itself plus one.

There is nothing _wrong_ with this argument. It shows a simple fact: if we enumerate a batch of functions $\underline{f}_1, \ldots, \underline{f}_i \ldots$, each of which attacks a natural number so as to come out with a unique result, then we can always find a new function which is not in the original enumeration.

The proof is simple, but we need now to point out what it has to do with "self-reference." In the proof just above we considered a function of _two arguments_, to wit, applying the _i_-th function to the number _j_. This is all perfectly straightforward as long as _i_ and _j_ are distinct; the pathological case arises from consideration of what happens when _i_ and _j_ are the same number, which is what we do in showing that the function _g_ _cannot_ be among the _f_'s. We _require_, for the argument, that we be able to apply the _i_-th function _to_ _its_ _own_ _index_ (or subscript).

If _this_ sort of self-reference were disallowed, we would lose virtually all of the most interesting fields in contemporary studies in the philosophical foundations of mathematics. The fundamental theorems of set-theory and of recursion theory would disappear, and mathematicians and logicians the world over would be out of business.

VI

The punch line seems then to be somewhat as follows.

(1) In some cases, those like the one just described, self-reference leads to interesting and fascinating mathematical theories (recursive functions, set theory), but

(2) when self-reference is applied to notions of truth and falsity in a sufficiently abandoned way, we get results which have proved to be puzzling for more than two millenia.

The papers to follow (to repeat the phrase with which I started) are devoted to saving us from the contradictions involved in (2), without sacrificing the beauties involved in (1).

I wish the contributors all good luck.

Truth and Paradoxical Consequences

by Bas C. van Fraassen

In a previous paper[1] I developed an approach to the semantic paradoxes based on Strawson's theory of presuppositions. Since then the work of Skyrms, Martin, and Herzberger has forced me to consider how this original rather modest proposal could be extended. In section I of this paper I will briefly recapitulate my earlier work, and give some new motivation. The limitations of the earlier treatment will be discussed in section II, and in sections III and IV some of these limitations will be removed.

I

A solution to the semantic paradoxes should presumably have two distinguishable parts: an analysis of the logically relevant features of the paradoxes as stated in natural language, and a formal construction in which corresponding sentences play roles roughly similar to those which our analysis ascribes to the paradoxical statements. (I say roughly, because the analysis may conceivably be successful even though it ignores various features of natural language.) To explain the solution I have proposed, I need to take up two preliminary subjects: presuppositions and truth-values.

Presuppositions

The notion of presupposition as a semantic relation among statements is best known from the writings of Strawson. The basic kind of example is:

> That the king of France is bald presupposes that the king of France exists.

The explicit characterization of this relation is then:

> A presupposes B if and only if A is true or false only if B is true.

1. B. C. van Fraassen, "Presupposition, Implication, and Self-Reference," Journal of Philosophy, 65 (1968), 136–52; henceforth [PRIM].

This becomes a very manageable relation if we assume the language to contain choice-negation: (not-$\underline{A}$) is true (false) if and only if $\underline{A}$ is false (true). For then this amounts to:

$\underline{A}$ presupposes $\underline{B}$ if and only if $\underline{A} \Vdash \underline{B}$ and (not-$\underline{A}$) $\Vdash \underline{B}$

where $\Vdash$, semantic entailment, is the relation which the premise(s) bear(s) to the conclusion in a valid argument. (Instead of "semantic entailment" I shall sometimes use "necessitation" for this relation.)

It will be clear that if every sentence is either true or false always, then presupposition is a trivial relation, being borne only to the universally valid sentences. So if we intend to hold that there are nontrivial cases of presupposition in a language, then we must construe this language as not bivalent.

Truth-values

Since I do hold that there are significant instances of presuppositions even in descriptive language, it follows that I do not construe language in the way the usual elementary logic text does. From this it should not be concluded that I reject the logic taught there. But the urgent question is: How do I propose to construe the language? My opinion is that language is essentially incomplete, in the sense that objective facts and conventions governing language do not suffice to determine the truth-value of every sentence.[2] Where they do suffice, they do so in just the manner spelled out in elementary logic. If we now wish to check a simple argument ($\underline{A}_1$, ..., $\underline{A}_n$; hence $\underline{B}$) we assume that the premises are true and see if it follows that the conclusion is true. In the preliminary assumption we may be assuming that some of the incompleteness has been eliminated in some way:[3] we direct ourselves to an ideal completion of the language. In general, when checking for validity, we have to consider all possible factual situations in relation to all (or arbitrary) ideal completions of the language. Thus in elementary cases, where the roles of the logical signs are all that is taken into account, the language is to be conceived of as bivalent. This "explains" why the usual truth-table methods are adequate for normal appraisal of reasoning.

2. Discussions with Karel Lambert, University of California at Irvine, and David Kaplan, University of California at Los Angeles, have helped to clarify this topic for me, and led me to the formulation which follows.

3. As the language evolves, this may indeed happen; and if some follower of Quine, abhorrent of vacua, were to be in charge of language reform, it would.

This will suggest how I would formally construe the language. A <u>classical</u> <u>valuation</u> is an assignment of T (true) or F (false) to each sentence, observing the usual truth-table rules for <u>or</u> and <u>not</u> and so on. Such an assignment will normally go far beyond what is actually true or false in a given situation, so a model of a factual situation (for a given language) is provided by the intersection of a class of classical valuations. This is called a <u>supervaluation</u>.

We may note that a sentence or argument in the language is valid under all supervaluations if and only if it is valid under all classical valuations. This justifies the acceptance of classical logic to appraise all reasoning in the language. But reasoning <u>about</u> the language will of course be affected. A specific example of this may be given with respect to the subject of truth itself. The argument from <u>A</u> to <u>It is true that</u> <u>A</u> is of course valid, as is the converse argument. But we shall in general reject the material equivalence of the two sentences, to block the inference from (<u>A</u> <u>or</u> <u>not-A</u>) to (<u>True</u> (<u>A</u>) <u>or</u> <u>True</u> (<u>not-A</u>)), because the former is valid even when neither <u>A</u> nor (<u>not-A</u>) is true.[4]

Paradoxes

Epimenides the Cretan stated that all Cretans are liars. If by this he meant that all their statements are false, then what he said could not be true, because then what he said entailed that what he said was false. But it could be false, and certainly it <u>would</u> be false if we found any statement by a Cretan that was true. The latter could clearly not be that very statement by Epimenides, for this would bring us back to the absurd first alternative. Thus what he said was false (if and) only if there exists another statement by a Cretan that is true.

What we have just done is to exhibit an empirical—and logically quite fallible—presupposition of what Epimenides said. This presupposition is that there exists some other statement by a Cretan that is true. Let us call it <u>Y</u>, and Epimenides' own statement <u>X</u>. The preceding paragraph establishes that if <u>X</u> is true, then everything (including <u>Y</u>) is true; and also that if <u>X</u> is false then <u>Y</u> is true. Thus by our definitions, <u>X</u> presupposes <u>Y</u>. In addition, by similar reasoning, <u>X</u> presupposes (not-<u>X</u>); and we note that if <u>Y</u> is true then <u>X</u> is false. So there are exactly two possibilities: the presupposition holds and <u>X</u> is false; or the presupposition fails. In the latter case, <u>X</u> is of course <u>neither</u> <u>true</u> <u>nor</u> <u>false</u>: that is what failure of a presupposition amounts to.

---

4. More specifically, $P \supset T(P)$ cannot be accepted as valid, but $T(P) \supset P$ may be so accepted without harm; see [PRIM], section III.

This is a solution, in the sense of an analysis which credits the Epimenidean statement with all the logical features that lead to the subordinate conclusions in the paradox, but blocks the final derivation of absurdity on general grounds concerning the structure of language. I have called this paradox the <u>Weakened Liar</u> because the statement can have a truth-value. The ordinary <u>Liar</u> is the statement "What I now say is false," which presupposes a contradiction, and hence cannot have a truth-value. The <u>Strengthened Liar</u> is a statement <u>X</u>, such that both it and <u>It is true that X</u> cannot have a truth-value. An example is the statement "What I now say is either false or neither true nor false." This classification seems to capture all the traditional semantic paradoxes, but of course from a logical point of view there is no finite limit on the iteration of "It is true that," so that we could produce also <u>Strengthened strengthened</u> . . . <u>strengthened Liars</u> (more about these later).[5]

How to Introduce Presuppositions

After this rather lengthy analysis, let us turn to the formal construction which is to show how things could possibly be the way we have said they are. Let our language have atomic sentences $\underline{p}, \underline{q}, \ldots$, unary connectives $\underline{T}, \sim$, and binary connective v. If $\underline{A}$, $\underline{B}$ are sentences so are $\underline{T}(\underline{A})$, $(\sim\underline{A})$, $(\underline{A} \text{ v } \underline{B})$. The classical valuations are just all the mappings v of the sentences into $\{T, F\}$ such that

$$v(\sim\underline{A}) = F \quad \text{iff} \quad v(\underline{A}) = T$$
$$v(\underline{A} \text{ v } \underline{B}) = F \quad \text{iff} \quad v(\underline{A}) = v(\underline{B}) = F$$

(It is possible to restrict this class so as to make various harmless principles about $\underline{T}$ valid; e.g. $\underline{T}(\underline{A}) \supset \underline{A}$, with $\supset$ defined as usual.) We write "$\underline{X} \text{ C } \underline{A}$" for "all classical valuations which satisfy the set $\underline{X}$ also satisfy $\underline{A}$." We now introduce a relation N of sentences (or sets of sentences) to sentences. If we wish $\underline{A}$ to presuppose $\underline{B}$, we choose N so that $\underline{A} \text{ N } \underline{B}$ and $(\sim\text{A}) \text{ N } \text{B}$. Because we wish the argument from $\underline{A}$ to $\underline{T}(\underline{A})$ to be valid, and conversely, we choose N such that for every sentence $\underline{A}$, $\underline{A} \text{ N } \underline{T}(\underline{A})$ and $\underline{T}(\underline{A}) \text{ N } \underline{A}$. Paradoxical sentences are produced by giving them the right presuppositions. Thus $\underline{p}$ becomes the ordinary Liar sentence by choosing N such that N $\underline{p} \text{ N } \underline{T}(\sim\underline{p})$ and $\underline{T}(\sim\underline{p}) \text{ N } \underline{p}$.

Now the "real" or "admissible" valuations for this language will be a certain class of supervaluations, chosen in such a way that

---

5. A detailed analysis beginning with the ordinary <u>Liar</u> and ending with the <u>Weakened Liar</u> is to be found in [PRIM], section IV.

if A N B then $A \Vdash B$ under these supervaluations. To single out such a class of supervaluations, we need two definitions:

(a) A set G of sentences is <u>saturated</u> iff it is satisfied by a classical valuation, closed under C and also under N.
(b) A supervaluation is induced by a set G of sentences iff it is the intersection of the class of classical valuations that satisfy G.

Now we restrict the admissible valuations to supervaluations induced by saturated sets.[6] It is routine to check whether the resulting language is as it should be. We are not spending much time on this because later on we shall do it for a much richer language.

II

We have now a sentence A such that A is neither true nor false and $T(A)$ is false, sentence B such that neither B nor $T(B)$ is false, but $T(T(B))$ is false, and so on. Let $T^0(A)$ be the sentence A and $T^{n+1}(A)$ be $T(T^n(A))$ for all nonnegative integers n. Then I shall call A a sentence of value-type n if n is the least integer such that $T^n(A)$ is true or false. (Note that if $T^n(A)$ is true, so is $T^m(A)$, for any integer m.) So if A is true or false, A is of value-type zero; if A is a sentence of a value-type higher than zero, then A is not true in an extended sense: $\sim T^n(A)$ is true for some $n > 0$.

As far as the preceding discussion goes, it might be held that each sentence A is of value-type n for some integer n. In that case, its truth or nontruth is expressed by some other true sentence of the language. But in the formal construction we can choose N in such a way that A N $\sim T^n(A)$ and $\sim T^n(A)$ N A for each positive integer n. In that case A has no integral value-type at all, for the typically paradoxical arguments:

$$T^n(A); \text{ hence } A; \text{ hence } \sim T^n(A)$$
$$\sim T^n(A); \text{ hence } A; \text{ hence } T^n(A)$$

establish that $T^n(A)$ is neither true nor false for each integer n. We shall say that A is of value-type ω in that case. There is no way to express the nontruth of paradoxical sentences of value-type

6. One might wish to restrict the set of admissible valuations still further. The policy of not accepting further restrictions is called the <u>radical</u> policy in "Presuppositions, Supervaluations, and Free Logic" (in K. Lambert, ed., <u>The Logical Way of Doing Things</u> [New Haven, Yale University Press, 1969]; henceforth [PRUF]).

ω in our formal language. We could introduce a new symbol $\underline{T}^{\omega}$ for this express purpose; but then we would also be able to introduce paradoxes of value-type $\omega + 1$.

Herzberger and DeSousa pointed out to me that infinite families of paradoxes may be generated by more mundane means. If we allow the designation of sentences by singular terms, and regard $\underline{T(A)}$ as the result of applying a predicate $\underline{T}$ to a singular term $(\underline{A})$ designating the sentence $\underline{A}$, this may happen. For let $\underline{b} = (\sim\underline{Tb})$ be true. By substitutivity of identity, so are $\underline{b} = (\sim\underline{T(\sim Tb)})$, $\underline{b} = (\sim\underline{T(\sim T(\sim Tb))})$, and so on. Now we have the paradoxical arguments

$$\underline{Tb}; \text{ hence } \underline{T(\sim Tb)}; \text{ hence } \sim\underline{Tb}$$
$$\sim\underline{Tb}; \text{ hence } \underline{T(\sim Tb)}; \text{ hence } \underline{Tb}$$

so $\underline{Tb}$ is neither true nor false; also

$$\underline{T(\sim Tb)}; \text{ hence } \sim\underline{Tb}; \text{ hence } \underline{Tb} \text{ [see above]}$$
$$\sim\underline{T(\sim Tb)}; \text{ hence } \sim\underline{Tb}; \text{ hence } \underline{T(\sim Tb)}$$

so $\underline{T(\sim Tb)}$ is neither true nor false; and so on.

It is important to note that this is not a paradox of type ω, since it is consistent with the above to hold for example that $\sim\underline{TTb}$ is true, so that $\underline{Tb}$ is a sentence of value-type 1. Similarly, we may hold that $\sim\underline{TT(\sim Tb)}$ is true, so $\sim\underline{Tb}$, i.e. $\underline{b}$, is a sentence of type 2. We $\underline{do}$ achieve the effect of a failure of bivalence at every syntactic level in this way (calling $\underline{A}$ a sentence of level $\underline{n}$ if the largest number of nested $\underline{T}$'s in $\underline{A}$ is $\underline{n}$). But we do not have a similar failure of our ability to express nontruth in the language.

Now Skyrms has questioned substitutivity of identity in this context.[7] This would prevent the above blossoming of truth-value gaps resulting from the substitution of $(\sim\underline{Tb})$ for $\underline{b}$. In fact, if $(\underline{A})$ is a name of $\underline{A}$, then the terms occurring with referential transparency in $\underline{A}$ will not (normally?) so occur in $(\underline{A})$. It would also allow us to say of a sentence $\underline{A}$ of value-type ω that it is not true: $\underline{b} = (\underline{A}) \& \sim\underline{Tb}$. I suffer from a clear lack of expressibility here, and I no longer find Skyrms' maneuver (also adopted by Herzberger) as counterintuitive as I once did. But the semantic problems involved in implementing this maneuver appear quite difficult, and for the time being I shall content myself with sacrificing the expressibility of the nontruth of paradoxical sentences of value-type ω.

A second, quite different possible objection to my approach is that the paradoxical sentences are not syntactically distinguished.

7. B. Skyrms, "Return of the Liar," commentary on J. Pollock's "The Truth about Truth," APA (Western Division), Chicago, May 1967.

The relation **N** (or the assignment of sentences as denotations to certain names) which produces the paradoxes may not be finitely or recursively specified. And even if it is, this may not be satisfactory: for in natural language, paradoxical sentences are generated by definite mechanisms, and there is general interest in the modeling of these mechanisms. The famous precedents here are those of combinatory logic, Raymond Smullyan, and Hans Reichenbach. This is a problem on which I have not worked at all.

Without denying the importance of this kind of problem, I would nevertheless like to argue the value of working on a more abstract level. By not being too definite on syntactic mechanisms, by relying on a quite shallow analysis of the grammatical structure, we can at least find out how much of the discussion of the paradoxes is really about the semantic relations among sentences. Presumably results on this level of generality will carry over to more specific cases as well. In the following section I shall introduce one mechanism producing self-reference: the denotation of sentences by names in the same language. And it will be seen that this is largely an application of previous techniques and results to a new case.

Before doing so, let us briefly consider what kinds of paradoxes may be so produced. If $\underline{b}$ denotes the sentence $\sim T\underline{b}$, then as we have seen, $\underline{b}$ is paradoxical of value-type 2, and $T\underline{b}$ paradoxical of value-type 1. If $\underline{b}$ denotes $\sim(T\underline{b} \ \& \ TT\underline{b})$, then $TT\underline{b}$ and $\sim TT\underline{b}$ both lead to a contradiction,[8] but $\sim TTT\underline{b}$ does not, so $\underline{b}$ is paradoxical of value-type 3. In this way we can produce paradoxes of any finite value-type. It does not seem, however, that we can produce paradoxes of value-type ω without introducing new predicates, or rather, without allowing the relation **N** to determine the extension of some predicate other than $\underline{T}$ in some farreaching way,[9] or using **N** to generate such a paradox directly as above. (It might be interesting to consider what kinds of syntactic mechanisms do produce infinitely paradoxical sentences.)

III

We are now going to discuss paradoxes formulated in a language with quantification, identity, and individual constants. To begin

8. $TTB \ |\!\!\vdash \ T\underline{b}, \ T\underline{b} \ |\!\!\vdash \ \sim(T\underline{b} \ \& \ TT\underline{b}); \ \sim TT\underline{b} \ |\!\!\vdash \ (\sim TT\underline{b} \ v \ \sim T\underline{b}), \ (\sim TT\underline{b} \ v \ \sim T\underline{b}) \ |\!\!\vdash \ \sim(T\underline{b} \ \& \ TT\underline{b}), \ \sim(T\underline{b} \ \& \ TT\underline{b}) \ |\!\!\vdash \ T \ (\sim(T\underline{b} \ \& \ TT\underline{b})), \ T \ (\sim(T\underline{b} \ \& \ TT\underline{b})) \ |\!\!\vdash \ T\underline{b}, \ T\underline{b} \ |\!\!\vdash \ TT\underline{b}$.

9. Let $\underline{Q}$ be a monadic predicate other than $\underline{T}$ and set $T^n\underline{B} \ \mathbf{N} \ \underline{Q}\underline{b}$ $(\sim T^n\underline{B}) \ \mathbf{N} \ (\underline{Q}\underline{b})$ for all integers n, and now let $\underline{b} = \sim\underline{Q}\underline{b}$.

I shall make some of the technical notions precise. In my termi-
nology, a <u>language</u> is an ordered pair $\underline{L}$ = <<u>Synt</u>, <u>Val</u>> where <u>Synt</u>
is a syntactic system and <u>Val</u> a set of valuations of <u>Synt</u> (the admissible valuations of $\underline{L}$). By a valuation I mean a mapping of
some of the sentences into the set $\{T, F\}$; the mapping need not be
defined for all sentences. A valuation satisfies a set $\underline{X}$ of sentences if it maps $\underline{X}$ into $\{T\}$, and satisfies a sentence $\underline{A}$ if it maps
$\{\underline{A}\}$ into $\{T\}$. $\underline{X} \Vdash \underline{A}$ holds in $\underline{L}$ if every admissible valuation of $\underline{L}$
which satisfies $\underline{X}$ also satisfies $\underline{A}$.

From now on, the syntax will be that of the language of quantification and identity theory: the logical signs are '&', '$\sim$', ')', '(',
'='; and there are predicates of all finite degrees, denumerably
many variables and denumerably many individual constants (names).
By a <u>sentence</u> I mean exactly what is also called a well-formed
formula, and by a <u>statement</u> I mean a sentence in which no variable
occurs free. Let $\underline{L}_0$ be the language which has this syntax and the
usual semantics: I shall assume that the reader knows which valuations of this syntax are the admissible valuations of $\underline{L}_0$.

Let us consider for a moment what it would mean to have a
truth-predicate in some language $\underline{L}$, applying to the name of a sentence just in case that sentence is true.

<u>Definition</u>:   In $\underline{L}$, monadic predicate $\underline{P}$ (<u>semantically</u>) <u>represents</u>
<u>truth with respect to</u> mapping $\underline{g}$ of the statements of
$\underline{L}$ into the names of $\underline{L}$ <u>for</u> a valuation $\underline{v}$ if and only if,
for any statement $\underline{A}$, $\underline{v(A)} = T$ if and only if $\underline{v(Pg(A))}$ =
T.

In addition we can say that $\underline{P}$ <u>strongly</u> <u>represents</u> <u>truth</u> <u>with</u> <u>respect</u>
<u>to</u> $\underline{g}$ if it does so for all admissible valuations of $\underline{L}$. The above is a
rather weak notion of representation; we could place further require-
ments on it such as that $\underline{v(Pg(A) \supset A)} = T$, or that $\underline{v(Pb)} = F$ (or, perhaps, not defined) when $\underline{b} \neq \underline{g(A)}$ for any sentence $\underline{A}$, and so on. In the
language which we shall construct, such conditions may be satisfied
by a suitable choice of the relation $\mathbf{N}$.

It will be clear that no predicate strongly represents truth in the
language $\underline{L}_0$, and that if $\underline{g(\sim Pb)} = \underline{b}$, for any name $\underline{b}$, then $\underline{P}$ does not
represent truth with respect to $\underline{g}$ for any admissible valuation. Our
aim is to construct a language $\underline{L}$ in which $\underline{P}$ (say, the first-monadic
predicate) strongly represents truth, without placing any restrictions
on $\underline{g}$.

To construct $\underline{L}$, we begin with $\underline{L}_0$, and add a relation N_0 of nonclassical necessitation. The admissible valuations of $\underline{L}_0$ will be the
classical valuations of $\underline{L}$, and the admissible valuations of $\underline{L}$ will be
the supervaluations induced by saturated sets of sentences, as above
(p. 17). Abbreviating $\underline{Pg(A)}$ henceforth as $\underline{T(A)}$, we require that N_0
be chosen such that, at least,

$$\underline{A} \; \mathbf{N}_0 \; \underline{T(A)}$$

$$\underline{T(A)} \; \mathbf{N}_0 \underline{A}$$

for every sentence $\underline{A}$. These are the minimal conditions on $\mathbf{N}_0$, and we shall call $\mathbf{N}_0$ minimal when these define it. We now have three results on $\underline{L}$, constructed in this manner.

Theorem 1: $\underline{P}$ strongly represents truth with respect to $\underline{g}$ in $\underline{L}$.

This follows because $\mathbf{N}_0$ was so chosen that $\underline{Pg(A)}$ and $\underline{A}$ semantically entail each other, for each sentence $\underline{A}$.

Theorem 2: $\underline{X} \Vdash \underline{A}$ holds in $\underline{L}$ if and only if $\underline{A}$ belongs to the smallest set of sentences of $\underline{L}$ containing $\underline{X}$ and closed under $\mathbf{N}_0$ and under the relation of semantic entailment in $\underline{L}_0$.

This is a special case of a previous result.[10] It shows that all classically valid statements and arguments are valid in $\underline{L}$. Also, it shows how to extend classical logic into a logical system sound and complete for $\underline{L}$ if the relation $\mathbf{N}_0$ can be specified in a suitable manner (as is the case if $\mathbf{N}_0$ is minimal, for example).

As an example we return to the case in which $\underline{b}$ denotes $\sim$(Tb & TTb). This means: $\underline{b} = \underline{g}(\sim\underline{(Pb} \, \& \underline{Pg} \, \underline{(Pb)}))$. Now $\underline{Pg(Pb)}$ entails both $\underline{Pb}$ and $\sim\underline{(Pb} \, \& \underline{Pg(Pb)})$. On the other hand, $\sim\underline{Pg(Pb)}$ entails classically $\sim\underline{(Pb} \, \& \, \underline{Pg(Pb)})$, and hence $\underline{Pg}(\sim\underline{(Pb} \, \& \, \underline{Pg(Pb)}))$, and so $\underline{Pb}$; but then also $\underline{Pg(Pb)}$.

The last theorem represents a new result, and it shows that a certain criterion of adequacy is met by our construction. This is the criterion that the introduction of paradoxical sentences should not make the language useless for ordinary purposes. Besides referring to sentences and ascribing truth or falsity, we may wish, say, to refer to knives and ascribe elegance, well-balancedness, sharpness, and so on. Factual situations ought to be describable in $\underline{L}$ as well as in $\underline{L}_0$. So let $\underline{SY}$ be the set of statements in which neither $\underline{P}$ nor any of the names $\underline{g(A)}$ occurs, and let $\mathbf{N}_0$ be minimal; paradoxes will then occur only in virtue of the mapping $\underline{g}$, and possibly the contingent truth of identity statements such as $\underline{b} = \underline{c}$ where $\underline{c}$ happens to be $\underline{g}(\sim\underline{Tb})$.

Theorem 3: If $\mathbf{N}_0$ is minimal, and $\underline{X}$ is a subset of $\underline{SY}$ satisfiable in $\underline{L}_0$, then $\underline{X}$ is satisfiable in $\underline{L}$.

10. [PRUF], Theorem 3. The adoption of the conservative instead of the radical policy for $\underline{L}$ would have yielded the same result if $\mathbf{N}_0$ is minimal, and a similar result for the general case; see [PRUF].

Proof: Let the antecedent hold, and let $\underline{X}^1$ be defined to be the infinite union of the sets $\underline{X}_i$, $\underline{i} = 1, 2, \ldots$, which are in turn defined by:

$$\underline{X}_1 = \underline{X}$$
$$\underline{X}_{2\underline{i}} = \{\underline{A}: \ \underline{X}_{2\underline{i}-1} \ \Vdash \underline{A} \ \text{in} \ \underline{L}_0\}$$
$$\underline{X}_{2\underline{i}+1} = \underline{X}_{2\underline{i}} \cup \{T(\underline{A}): \ \underline{A} \in \underline{X}_{2\underline{i}}\}.$$

We intend to prove that $\underline{X}^1$—and hence its subset $\underline{X}$—is satisfiable in $\underline{L}$.

To establish this, note that $\underline{X}^1$ is closed under both classical and nonclassical necessitation, for $\Vdash$ in $\underline{L}_0$ is finitary, and so is the minimal N_0. Hence if in addition $\underline{X}^1$ is satisfiable in $\underline{L}_0$, then $\underline{X}^1$ is a saturated set and will induce an admissible (super)valuation, which satisfies it in $\underline{L}$. Thus it remains only to show that $\underline{X}^1$ is satisfiable in the classical language $\underline{L}_0$.

As a preliminary, we point out that if $\underline{B}$ is a member of $\underline{X}_{2\underline{i}}$, for given $\underline{i}$, then there are statements $\underline{A}_1, \ldots, \underline{A}_m$ in $\underline{X} = \underline{X}_1$ and $T(\underline{A}_{m+1}), \ldots, T(\underline{A}_n)$ in $\underline{X}_{2\underline{i}-1}$ such that $\underline{A}_1, \ldots, \underline{A}_m, T(\underline{A}_{m+1}), \ldots, T(\underline{A}_n) \Vdash \underline{B}$ in $\underline{L}_0$. This can be proved by induction: clearly it holds for $\underline{i} = 1$, because $\underline{X}_2 = \{\underline{A}: \underline{X}_1 \Vdash \underline{A} \ \text{in} \ \underline{L}_0\}$ and $\Vdash$ in $\underline{L}_0$ is finitary, so there will be $\underline{A}_1, \ldots, \underline{A}_m$ in $\underline{X}_1$ such that $\underline{A}_1, \ldots, \underline{A}_m \Vdash \underline{B}$ if $\underline{B}$ is in $\underline{X}_2$ (let $\underline{n} = \underline{m}$, i.e. $\{T(\underline{A}_{m+1}), \ldots, T(\underline{A}_n)\}$ is empty here). Suppose now that we have proved it for $\underline{i} = \underline{n}$, and let $\underline{B}$ be a member of $\underline{X}_{2(\underline{n}+1)} = X_{2n+2}$. Then, by the finitary character of $\Vdash$ in $\underline{L}_0$, there are sentences $\underline{A}_1, \ldots, \underline{A}_n$ of $\underline{X}_{2n+1}$ such that $\underline{A}_1, \ldots, \underline{A}_n \Vdash \underline{B}$ in $\underline{L}_0$. Now $\underline{X}_{2n+1}$ is the union of $\underline{X}_{2n}$ and $T(\underline{A}): \{\underline{A} \in \underline{X}_{2n}\}$. So let $\underline{A}_1, \ldots, \underline{A}_m$ be in $\underline{X}_{2n}$ and $\underline{A}_{m+1} = T(\underline{A}^*_{m+1}), \ldots, \underline{A}_n = T(\underline{A}^*_n)$ be in $\underline{X}_{2n+1} - \underline{X}_{2n}$. By the hypothesis of induction, there are sentences $\underline{A}^1_1, \ldots, \underline{A}^1_{m_1}, \ldots, \underline{A}^m_1, \ldots, \underline{A}^m_{n_m}$ and $T(\underline{A}^1_1), \ldots, T(\underline{A}^1_{n_1}), \ldots, T(\underline{A}^m_1), \ldots, T(\underline{A}^m_{n_m})$ such that $\underline{A}^{\underline{i}}_{\underline{l}}$ is in $\underline{X}$ and $\{\underline{A}^{\underline{i}}_{\underline{l}}, T(\underline{A}^{\underline{i}}_{\underline{l}})\} \Vdash \underline{A}_i$, for $\underline{i} = 1, \ldots, \underline{m}$; $\underline{l} = 1, \ldots, \underline{m}_i$; $\underline{l} = 1, \ldots, \underline{n}_i$. By the transitivity of semantic entailment, we see that the set $\{\underline{A}^{\underline{i}}_{\underline{l}}\} \subseteq \underline{X}$ together with $\{T(\underline{A}^{\underline{i}}_{\underline{l}})\} \cup \{T(\underline{A}^*_{m+1}), \ldots, T(\underline{A}^*_n)\} \subseteq \underline{X}_{2n+1}$ semantically entails $\underline{B}$ in $\underline{L}_0$ (with the indices as before). This proves our preliminary claim.

Now suppose, per absurdum, that $\underline{X}^1$ is not satisfiable in $\underline{L}_0$. Then it contains a contradiction $(Q \ \& \sim Q)$; and this contradiction must belong to $\underline{X}_{2\underline{i}}$ for some index $\underline{i}$. By the preceding paragraph there must then be sentences $\underline{A}_1, \ldots, \underline{A}_m$ in $\underline{X}$ and $\underline{Pb}_1, \ldots, \underline{Pb}_n$ in $\underline{X}_{2\underline{i}-1}$, such that $\underline{A}_1, \ldots, \underline{A}_m, \underline{Pb}_1, \ldots, \underline{Pb}_n \Vdash (Q \ \& \sim Q)$

in $\underline{L}_0$. This is equivalent to: $\underline{A}_1, \ldots, \underline{A}_m \Vdash \sim (\underline{Pb}_1 \& \ldots \& \underline{Pb}_n)$ in $\underline{L}_0$. Since $\underline{A}_1, \ldots, \underline{A}_m$ belong to $\underline{\underline{X}}$, and hence to $\underline{SY}$, it follows that the antecedent and consequent here have no nonlogical signs in common. So by Craig's Lemma, either the conjunction of the antecedent $(\underline{A}_1 \& \ldots \& \underline{A}_m)$ is a contradiction, or the consequent is a tautology. The former cannot be because $\underline{X}$ is satisfiable in $\underline{L}_0$, and the latter cannot be because a conjunction of atomic sentences $\underline{Pb}_1 \& \ldots \& \underline{Pb}_n$ is never a contradiction. So $\underline{X}^1$ must be satisfiable in $\underline{L}_0$ after all, and this finishes the proof.

In conclusion, the one limitation that I have not removed is that the nontruth of a sentence of value-type ω cannot be expressed in the formal languages constructed. This is an objection against the claim that this construction provides a model for the relevant parts of natural language. There are ways to remedy this, but the remedy usually provides us with the resources for constructing further paradoxes, which yield new limitations on our means of expression. The exception to this seems to be the maneuver of placing restrictions on the substitutivity of identity; and the semantic rationale for this is presently being explored.[11]

11. This paper now seems much more limited in scope than it did at the time of writing; see my "Inference and Self-Reference" (forthcoming in Synthese). Specifically, the syntactic mechanisms for production of self-reference do not all fall so neatly in the classical mold as does reference to sentences by means of constants occurring in those sentences.

Truth and Modality in Semantically Closed Languages

by Hans G. Herzberger

Supervaluations

Van Fraassen's theory of presuppositional languages,[1] based on the method of supervaluations, strikes a path through a logical jungle bristling with pitfalls and wild beasts. Its artful blending of classical proof theory and nonclassical semantics opens new directions and reopens old ones that long have been overgrown with forgotten tangles.

For more than forty years, three-valued logic was basically the Łukasiewicz system, of which Storrs McCall has said that "it contains all of the vices and none of the virtues of two-valued logic." McCall's own opinion is:

> These defects of three-valued logic arise not from its three-valuedness but from its truth-functional character . . . . It would be perfectly possible to have a logic that was three-valued without being truth-functional.[2]

And now we have it, in the method of supervaluations.[3] We have it furthermore applied to the paradoxes in connection with a new theory of truth that weakens the relation between a sentence k and the sentence saying that k is true. On the classical correspondence theory the relation is one of coimplication, and on this new theory it is one of conecessitation.

Alternatives to the correspondence theory are sorely wanted on account of the semantic paradoxes, which on the whole are log-

1. As developed in the cited papers culminating in his contribution [TPC] to this volume. (Bracketed abbreviations refer to list of references at the end of this paper.)

2. In McCall, [TF], 278. Also, A. Prior has written: "The truth-functional technique seems simply out of place here" [PPF], 135.

3. The sense in which this system is trivalent and not truth-functional should become evident as the discussion proceeds. In particular its trivalence rests on a threefold partition of sentences into true, false, and neither — a structural property independent of any further distinctions to be drawn between the absence of a standard truth-value and the presence of a nonstandard truth-value.

ical symptoms of the profound inadequacy of that theory. The long development of logic in its shadow has rendered it so powerful a tradition that it grips one in the very process of being shaken off. From this standpoint van Fraassen's alternative emerges as a milestone marking a halfway point in the process. After surveying it I propose to contrast it with another view that is initially more radical but that ultimately may achieve a fuller integration of semantic principles and intuitions. I hope this contrast will sharpen our understanding of both alternatives; and in any case a theory as elegant and powerful as van Fraassen's can hardly be tested except by confrontation with another theory. Since Skyrms and Martin each build on supervaluations in their separate ways, their theories will not serve my end. That is my excuse for multiplying theories perhaps beyond some necessity in this volume.

Degrees of Semantic Closure

Progress on the Liar paradox is progress in our theory of semantically closed languages. History indicates that the Liar may never wholly be laid to rest, and so progressive criteria marking levels of success may be appropriate. The guiding idea is that of a language capable of reflecting the principles and details of its own semantic structure. Increasing capacity in this regard can be marked in terms of atomic, molecular, and general semantic propositions:

Atomic Closure:	L contains the means for recording the truth-value of each of its own sentences.
Molecular Closure:	L contains the means for expressing all singular consequences of its semantic theory.
General Closure:	L contains the means for expressing the whole of its own semantic theory.

The first two levels are related, I believe, to Tarski's criterion of incorporating a truth-predicate and Skyrm's criterion of incorporating a "mildly global" truth-predicate (whose extension consists of exactly the true sentences, and whose category furthermore consists of all sentences).[4]

The first connection is straightforward: given truth, falsity can be defined as truth of the negation, and nonstandard truth-values can be predicated by way of extra primitives, or even repudiated as philosophically repugnant.

4. Tarski, [SCT], n. 8; Skyrms, [RL].

Smullyan's investigations have made it clear that the paradoxes engage the notion of truth only indirectly; it is after all non-truth in the first instance that is elusive.[5] The sentence that denies truth of itself is not true, and this fact of semantic structure may resist formulation in languages of the first degree of semantic closure. Tarski's criterion in retrospect presumed definability of all other semantic concepts in terms of truth, a reasonable presumption in bivalent frameworks. Once truth-value gaps are admitted however, alongside the categories of truth and falsity there arises that category of "indeterminate" sentences that are neither true nor false. It then emerges that the two forms of nontruth (falsity and indeterminacy) mix uneasily, and interdefinability of logical categories can no longer be taken for granted. Thus Skyrm's criterion, which in effect requires the concept of nontruth alongside the concept of truth.

From a logical standpoint, the second degree of closure is marked by the emergence of two negation-like connectives, commonly known as choice- and exclusion-negation, which I prefer to have known as negation and complementation respectively:

(Choice) Negation		Complementation	
P	~P	P	P̄
T	F	T	F
F	T	F	T
I	I	I	T

The former allows falsity to be defined in terms of truth, and the latter allows both nontruth and indeterminacy to be defined in terms of truth as well. To connect these features now with my second degree of closure, consider the principle that only determinate sentences are true. Schematically this has the singular molecular consequence: If k is indeterminate then k is not true. And a mildly global truth-predicate seems required in order to admit the formulation of all such singular consequences of the semantic theory. Negation without complementation shields falsity and indeterminacy from one another, purchasing logical consistency on a note of expressive incompleteness.

The second degree of semantic closure is designed to render a language capable of expressing each particular fact of its semantic structure, but not thereby the general principles of its semantic theory. It guarantees a truth-predicate whose behavior with singular terms is exemplary, but is not fully adequate in that it permits

5. Smullyan, [TFS], ch. 3-A, and [LSRP].

a truth-predicate whose behavior with bound variables is disappointing. The next level of success that might be envisaged then is a theory of languages admitting of general semantic closure.

The schematic character of these three conditions should not go unremarked. The rub is that any theory of semantically closed languages is bound to incorporate a nonclassical model theory of its own design, in terms of which its own adequacy is to be assessed, thus rendering such assessment a delicate matter. The guiding idea of a language sufficiently rich to reflect the whole of its semantic structure should always be kept in view. As they stand, however schematically, these conditions do impose very palpable constraints that serve to guide investigation.

Other constraints along with these are welcome. For those with an eye to natural language, compatibility with what is known of transformational grammar might occasionally be brought to bear in adjudicating otherwise undecidable issues. Another guideline is a Quine-like logical conservatism implemented in a striking way here by van Fraassen: one holds to orthodox proof theory at least in its main outlines, and grafts onto it a novel semantics. This direction and these priorities seem to me eminently worth following, and I think one might go even farther than van Fraassen does in taming and domesticating the third truth-value.

Trivalent Connectives

I spoke earlier of pitfalls and wild beasts. The pitfalls in trivalent semantics are the loss of some classically valid theorems and inferences. On this point the supervaluation approach comes out well: proof theory is redeemed, as Skyrms puts it, from the Fregean notion of Sin.[6]

Secondly there are the wild beasts. Any trivalent logic that hankers after functional completeness must embrace what van Fraassen calls "wonderful new connectives" that defy interpretation.[7] On this second problem also the supervaluation approach comes out quite well, although here I think there is room for improvement on two counts.

The number of connectives is not increased, but their interpretation is altered. Connectives are no longer truth-functional in the usual sense. They are however truth-relational, and they do impose fairly tight constraints on the truth-values of compound sentences. Skeletal matrices can be provided for them, to yield a fairly clear picture of the logical structure envisaged for super-

6. Skyrms, [S], 479.
7. Van Fraassen, [PSF], 69.

valuational languages. In these matrices, '$\overline{F}$' stands for nonfalse, '$\overline{T}$' stands for nontrue, and 'U' is a place-holder meaning value unspecified:

van Fraassen's Connectives

&	T	F	I		V	T	F	I		⊃	T	F	I		≡	T	F	I
T	T	F	I		T	T	T	T		T	T	F	I		T	T	F	I
F	F	F	F		F	T	F	I		F	T	T	T		F	F	T	I
I	I	F	$\overline{T}$		I	T	I	$\overline{F}$		I	T	I	$\overline{F}$		I	I	I	U

The matrices indicate that failures of truth-functionality are confined to the lower right-hand corners, which are the only places where symbols for composite values appear. I find a slight discrepancy with intuition in the biconditional matrix, whose corner is totally unspecified. This means that the biconditional does not appear to express material equivalence within this theory, for supervaluations allow a biconditional to be <u>false</u> even though its components are materially equivalent — in this case, both indeterminate. So at least one of van Fraassen's connectives is, if not a wild beast, at least not fully domesticated; as I should say, not quite housebroken. As to truth-functionality it seems to me better to have it than not, but one could live without it if all else were well.

A second discrepancy in this theory is the absence of one highly domesticated connective which is, when available, something of a beast of burden. This is Bochvar's generalization of Frege's horizontal, which to some minds is part and parcel of the concept of truth.[8]

Bochvar–Frege Horizontal

P	hP
T	T
F	F
I	F

Nothing like it can be had without some reconstrual of the substitutivity of identicals, which I will discuss in a wider context presently. On this point van Fraassen diverges deliberately from

---

8. Bochvar's version of the horizontal fills in truth-value gaps; Frege's, being closely tied to his <u>Begriffschrift</u>, becomes somewhat problematic in application to semantically closed languages (see Frege, [BL], 38, fn. 15.)

those of us who hold substitutivity negotiable.[9] Along with the horizontal, van Fraassen repudiates complementation, which is just (choice-)negation of the horizontal. This locates van Fraassen's theory with respect to Smullyan's classification of semantically closed languages into those that fail of what he calls "normality" and those that fail of complementation;[10] it also shows that van Fraassen's theory of truth falls short of the second level of semantic closure.

Natural Language

I want to remark very briefly on the evaluation of this framework as a theory of the semantic structure of natural language. On the assumption that a transformational grammar provides a theory of sense for sentences of a given language, and that the sense of any sentence determines both its conditions of determinateness and its conditions of truth, it is natural to expect the notion of "referential position" to be marked in such a theory as a grammatical feature of nounphrases somewhat on a par with features like "Singular," "Abstract," "Inanimate," and the rest. Quinians and Fregeans alike require systematic indication of the referential status of a nounphrase, and this does seem to be governed by grammatical features of the surrounding sentence. For example the sentence 'The whale is a mammal' is free on at least one reading of the kind of denotational presuppositions that are in force in the sentence 'The whale veered abruptly off course'. Verbal auxiliaries, adverbs, quotation marks, and specific verbs of propositional attitude are some of the grammatical indicators that override denotational presuppositions. It is natural therefore to have these distinctions marked by the presence or absence of a grammatical feature "Referential" on nounphrase positions within sentences. It seems clear however that van Fraassen's semantics is inconsistent with such a course, for his principle of redemption in effect holds the referential status of a singular term position subject to the classical validity or contravalidity of the surrounding sentence. But transformational grammars are decidable systems, and classical validity is not a decidable notion. This occasions a sharp confrontation between van Fraassen's semantic theory and transformational grammar; and on this point something is going to have to yield somewhere.

9. Van Fraassen, [TPC], 18.

10. Some caution is needed here on account of the inherent bivalence of languages in Smullyan's account.

Trivalent Modalities

Having surveyed this theory, let me now briefly sketch an alternative framework based on ideas of Buridan, Frege, and Bochvar which embodies a different method of dealing with the problems and intuitions underlying the supervaluation approach—this time by way of a more thoroughgoing restructuring of the correspondence theory of truth.

In discussing the Insolubilia, Jean Buridan remarked that "those propositions are indeed in conflict with regard to being true, but they are not in conflict with regard to the case being as they signify."[11] Put more positively, the case may be as a sentence signifies, and yet the sentence not be true. I read this to mean that correspondence conditions can be satisfied independently of presuppositions. Indeed this seems to be the case. The Liar sentence is not true, but that's exactly what it says, thereby engendering that all too familiar semantic collision between a component of veracity and a component of nonveracity in the same sentence.

Bivalent semantics imposes an either-or resolution of such conflicts. Thus in confronting analytic singular sentences like 'The golden mountain is golden', Meinong clings to the component of veracity, and Russell to the component of nonveracity. Neither alternative seems altogether felicitous, and Frege, Strawson, and others choose to reject both. A resolution of these conflicts along the lines of Buridan's semantics would, I believe, attempt to reconcile, rather than reject, both intuitions.

Let us say that a sentence is <u>secure</u> in case "things are as the sentence signifies," and <u>contrasecure</u> otherwise. If furthermore the requisite presuppositions are satisfied, the sentence will be true in the former case and false in the latter. Security then, which is my term for "correspondence with reality," is a constituent of truth—but not the whole of it. A partial representation of these categories can be obtained within trivalent semantics, with nonfalsity and nontruth as the trivalent counterparts of security and contrasecurity respectively.[12] Proceeding on this assumption, let

11. Buridan, [SMT], 183.

12. In the technical sense of D. Lewis [CT] in which a counterpart of a given thing within an alternative framework is something that resembles the given thing more closely than does anything else in that framework. Since this paper was written it has emerged, under criticism by Skyrms and van Fraassen, that while "nonfalse" can simulate "secure" for certain purposes, the resemblance in their behavior breaks down for other purposes, and that a quadrivalent rather than a trivalent framework may ultimately be more congenial to a full reconstruction of Buridan's semantics. I have discussed these issues under the title "Buridan and Two-Dimensional Model Theory" in a seminar on many-valued logic at Waterloo University, and will pursue them in detail in a forthcoming work.

us see how these distinctions can be applied to the resolution of semantic collisions.

The doctrine that necessary truth is a simple thing has penetrated our thinking to such an extent as to be canonized in our terminology. Logically valid sentences are called simply "logical truths," and analytic sentences are called simply "analytic truths." The time has come to reconsider that doctrine. Necessary truth is a modality carried over from orthodox semantics and imposed upon trivalent theories; but such imposition works a failure of parity into the treatment of contingent and necessary sentences. If correspondence conditions can be met independently of presuppositions in the one case, they can and more so in the other.

In bivalent semantics a sentence is always true, always false, or else contingent. Trivalent semantics admits of several more modalities, of which "never false" and "never true" deserve special consideration. They are the trivalent modal counterparts of security and contrasecurity. Logical security rather than logical truth seems to me to be what logically valid sentences have; analytic security rather than analytic truth seems to me to be what analytic sentences have. Necessity altogether seems to me a matter of security rather than a matter of truth; necessary truth seems to me not a simple thing but rather a composite of necessary security and satisfied presuppositions.

These considerations suggest a many-valued logic with security replacing truth as designated value. Beginning with Łukasiewicz' trivalent matrices and taking nonfalsehood as the designated value, peculiar things happen; but this I think is due to the peculiarities of the matrices themselves. In 1938 D. A. Bochvar proposed a quite different and very simple system of trivalent matrices, on two levels:[13]

Bochvar's "Internal" Connectives

&	T	F	I		V	T	F	I		⊃	T	F	I		≡	T	F	I
T	T	F	I		T	T	T	I		T	T	F	I		T	T	F	I
F	F	F	I		F	T	F	I		F	T	T	I		F	F	T	I
I	I	I	I		I	I	I	I		I	I	I	I		I	I	I	I

13. In Bochvar, [TVC]; compare Smiley's [SWD]. Kleene [IM] also employs the internal connectives (which he calls "weak" connectives) in a rather different context.

What Bochvar called "internal" connectives are given their matrices by assigning the third truth-value uniformly all along the border; negation here is choice-negation. With regard to presuppositions, "internal" connectives make no contribution at all; the presuppositions of an "internal" molecular compound are exactly those contributed by its component sentences. In addition to these connectives so construed, the horizontal completes the system and implements a systematic filling-in of truth-value gaps by way of the definition of an associated set of "external connectives." For example the "external negation" of $\underline{P}$ is complementation ($\sim\underline{h}\ \underline{P}$), and the "external conditional" of $\underline{P}$ and $\underline{Q}$ is ($\underline{hP} \supset \underline{hQ}$). Reading $\underline{hP}$ as the "external form of $\underline{P}$" Bochvar remarks: "Really these external forms represent nothing but corresponding internal forms into which are substituted the corresponding external propositions" ([TVC], p. 288). The primary concern here is not with these so-called external connectives but rather with the logic resulting from the standard connectives internally construed, along with free use of the horizontal.

Some initial resistance to the internal matrices may be overcome by a bit of historical explanation. The matrices to be found in Frege's logical theory are not for pure connectives, but rather for connectives thoroughly intercalated with horizontals; on this point of "amalgamation of horizontals" he is absolutely clear.[14] Frege offered no explanation for the pure connectives in isolation from the horizontals, nor is there reason to suppose he saw the need for such an explanation, which Bochvar's internal matrices undertake to provide.[15] Rather than explaining 'not', Frege explained the composite 'it is not the case that'; and the latter has come down to us tied to the negation-sign. Rather than explaining 'or', Frege explained the composite 'it is the case that . . . or it is the case that. . .'; and the latter has come down to us tied to the disjunction-sign. In Frege's notation the connectives clearly exhibit their composite structure, a feature soon lost under transition to the Russell notation. Thus our feeling of uneasiness in seeing the Bochvar internal matrices in explanation for the con-

---

14. In [BL], p. 40, n. 6 Frege writes: "Hence we regard '⊤' as composed of the small vertical stroke, the negation-stroke, and the two portions of the horizontal stroke, each of which may be regarded as horizontals in our sense." Compare also the remarks in [BL], pp. 43 and 51, on the quantifier and the conditional.

15. This is also Bochvar's claim: "The classical calculus . . . introduces only internal assertion and should therefore be semantically interpreted with the aid of internal forms" [TVC], 289.

nectives: we have forgotten the separate parts which Frege amalgamated and Russell fused together. The Bochvar "external" matrices fit our notation better, but in so doing they show how inadequate that notation is to the meaning of 'not', 'or', and the rest. Our notation is geared to bivalence, under which these distinctions collapse. In semantically closed languages bivalence is not to be had, and this forces upon us the separate analysis of logical connectives and semantic predicates that Frege failed to provide.

In Fregean semantics a sentence is determinate if and only if each of its singular terms has a denotation. This means that a molecular compound should be determinate if and only if each of its component sentences is determinate. With regard to denotational presuppositions then it is worth remarking that Bochvar's internal matrices would result from superimposing the Fregean principle of determinateness over the standard bivalent matrices.

Bochvar's own system lacks a prominent virtue of the supervaluation approach; his proof theory is nowhere near classical. The fault however may be not in his matrices but rather in his concept of validity: he follows the orthodox course of designating only truth. Taking nonfalsity as designated value yields the encouraging result that the internal system so understood exactly preserves the classically valid sentences. Buridan together with Bochvar then makes an interesting combination.[16]

Deduction of course no longer preserves truth, but truth-preservation again is a criterion carried over from bivalent semantics, and is eminently negotiable in connection with semantically closed languages. Van Fraassen has a footnote on this matter, in which he remarks that "it would be interesting to investigate the properties of those transformations that . . . at least do not take a truth into a falsehood."[17] Accordingly then, deduction within the Bochvar–Buridan system might be based on the following stipulation:

BB-Consequence: An argument is valid within the BB-system if and only if there is no valuation which jointly renders its premisses true and its conclusion false.

The guiding idea behind this enterprise is that validity and soundness of arguments rest on different grounds: validity is formal and soundness in the general case is material. Presuppositions,

16. Taking both truth and indeterminacy as designated values does not commit this theory to the absurdity that all indeterminate sentences are assertable, for the view that designated values mark assertable sentences is precisely the view being rejected here.

17. Van Fraassen, [STF], 483, fn. 2.

being of the latter sort, are well relegated to the theory of soundness and expurgated from the theory of validity. Once it is recognized that determinateness is not in general preserved under deduction, it is natural to enrich the notion of soundness so that a sound argument is taken to be one that is valid, has true premisses, and a determinate conclusion. Even in van Fraassen's system determinateness is not always preserved under deduction, for contradictions in that system imply any sentence, even an indeterminate one.

Of a piece then are Bochvar's internal matrices, the sharp conception of logical validity, and the weak interpretation of deduction. All result from a separation of presuppositions from correspondence conditions, and all are tied to Buridan's observation that the latter can be satisfied independently of the former.

Transcendence by Semantic Ascent

Turning finally from the language of the jungle to the language of theology, a semantic theory adequate to these conceptions might be based on semantic original Sin combined with Redemption on a different liturgical ground. According to the Gnostic theology, redemption comes to the children of darkness through an experience of union with their doppelgängers among the children of light. Internal connectives to some minds may be children of darkness, but as Bochvar and others have made clear, their doppelgängers among the external connectives are to be had as soon as the Bochvar–Frege horizontal can be expressed.[18] More generally the principal celestial redeemer in semantic theory seems to be, in spite of all resistance to it, transcendence by semantic ascent.

Theological imagery here fits the semantic idea very well. Truth can be affirmed or denied on such a view only from on high; in order to predicate truth of a sentence or set of sentences, some way must be found to rise above them. Paradoxes emerge where circumstances apparently prevent such transcendence, the most immediately impressive such case being direct self-reference. Under such circumstances artful maneuvers and uncommon devices are in order. Skyrms found a way to transcendence that achieves the second level of semantic closure, and Katz and I found the same way promising in our work on natural language.[19] It is implemented by negotiating the strong construal of consequence (as truth-preservation) in favor of the Bochvar–Frege horizontal along with some weaker construal of consequence.

18. Bochvar, [TVC], Part I-1; also Smiley, [SWD], Matheson, [SST], and Skyrms, [S], particularly on the redemption of negative existentials.
19. Skyrms, [RL], and Herzberger and Katz, [CTNL].

Repudiation of the correspondence theory of truth to the extent of tolerating exceptions to the equivalence-principle[20] leads in diverse ways to the first level of semantic closure. Devices to achieve transcendence in pathological circumstances furthermore illuminate the way to the second level of semantic closure. From this prospect the third level seems ever more remote, for semantic ascent when strictly enforced clearly would bar the formulation of fully general semantic principles as truths of any language they govern. Two ways then diverge from this point toward the third level: either a tolerance for restrictions on the rule of transcendence, or a stoical acceptance of bounds on what a language can truly express. The first path being rather too thorny to hazard here, let it suffice to indicate the viability of the stoical one.

Perhaps the general principles of semantic theory are simply not true; perhaps they go the way of analytic and logical truths, for essentially the same reason. A radical suggestion, but one coherent and unified with all that has gone before. Once one thinks of it, necessity without truth might well be exactly what those general principles have. They are at any rate inherently secure. On the strict transcendence view they would be not determinate and thereby not true.

A case in point is the equivalence-principle itself. On the projected account this principle is inherently secure, as are each of the Tarski biconditionals that can be derived as instances of it. Bochvar's internal matrices then yield the satisfactory result that indeterminate sentences uniformly have indeterminate Tarski biconditionals, whereas determinate sentences uniformly have true Tarski biconditionals.[21] The Liar paradox arises under circumstances that secure the negation of some Tarski biconditional, and thereby afford a ready proof of the indeterminacy of the offending sentence. The sharpness and simplicity of this account of the Liar paradox could be claimed to support the general view from which it flows. This view aims to preserve orthodox proof theory and orthodox semantics by a single device: construing all of their principles as necessarily secure, but neither necessarily nor even materially true.

20. That is, the doctrine that any sentence is materially equivalent to a canonical sentence saying that it is true — formulated with the horizontal as $[P \equiv hP]$.

21. In sharp contrast to Tarski's claim in [SCT], 362, that any theory rejecting the equivalence-principle is committed to <u>accepting</u> the negation of at least one Tarski biconditional, exemplified by the case [The sentence 'Snow is white' is true if and only if snow is not white). On van Fraassen's theory some Tarski biconditionals do come out false, but still not in connection with object-level sentences like 'Snow is white'.

In conclusion, supervaluations provide one liturgy of redemption and semantic ascent another. Van Fraassen adopts the first, Skyrms accepts them both at least in limited form, and I have sketched a proposal under which the latter takes over the whole work of redemption. In so doing it provides a unified theory which goes about as far in explaining the peculiarities of semantically closed languages as present knowledge admits. It shows a way to transcend particular expressive gaps by providing for each sentence lost through Fregean or Epimenidean Sin at least one doppelgänger that is redeemed. For the irredeemable it provides a secondary mode of expression by way of schemata that are necessarily secure although not determinate. Any such schema encapsulates a progression of determinate but more limited principles of endlessly increasing scope. This fits the view that some things can be said whereas other things can only be shown.

Appendix on the Bochvar-Buridan System[22]

A more precise account of the Bochvar-Buridan system is undertaken here in two stages. First the logical behavior of the system is studied for a first-degree semantically closed language that takes only the classical logical connectives into account. Then its behavior is studied for an expanded language that includes a greater portion of its own semantics by way of the Bochvar-Frege horizontal. Each language is given a double interpretation to facilitate comparison of the BB-system with classical logical theory.

The "Internal" Language L

Let the language $\underline{L}$ be composed of a set of atomic sentences along with the standard propositional connectives. Two sorts of bases for the semantic evaluation of $\underline{L}$ are defined:

A $\underline{b}$-model of $\underline{L}$ is any function $\underline{b}$ assigning exactly one of the three values $\{\underline{T}, \underline{F}, \underline{I}\}$ to each atomic sentence of the language $\underline{L}$.

A classical model of $\underline{L}$ is any fully bivalent $\underline{b}$-model, assigning exactly one of the two values $\{\underline{T}, \underline{F}\}$ to each atomic sentence of $\underline{L}$.

Each model now determines a valuation of the corresponding sort, which is a function defined over all sentences of $\underline{L}$:

---

22. I am greatly indebted to Skyrms and van Fraassen for critical discussions that led to this appendix by way of the result [T17].

The $\underline{b}$-valuation determined by any $\underline{b}$-model $\underline{b}$ is a function $\underline{Vb}$ whose value $\underline{Vb}(\underline{s})$ for any sentence $\underline{s}$ is reckoned according to Bochvar's internal matrices for the propositional connectives.

The classical valuation determined by any classical model $\underline{c}$ is a function $\underline{Vc}$ whose value $\underline{Vc}(\underline{s})$ for any sentence $\underline{s}$ is reckoned according to the standard two-valued matrices for the propositional connectives.

> $\underline{T}$ 1: A sentence is bivalent under any $\underline{b}$-valuation $\underline{Vb}$ iff the associated model $\underline{b}$ is bivalent over each of the atomic constituents of that sentence.

This is immediate by inspection of the internal matrices, for any Bochvar internal compound will have the value $\underline{I}$ iff at least one of its constituents has that value.

> $\underline{T}$ 2: For any sentence $\underline{s}$ and any $\underline{b}$-valuation $\underline{Vb}$ that renders it bivalent, there is a classical valuation $\underline{Vb}*$ such that $\underline{Vb}*(\underline{s}) = \underline{Vb}(\underline{s})$.

Form the valuation $\underline{Vb}*$ by setting $\underline{b}*(\underline{x}) = \underline{b}(\underline{x})$ for each atomic constituent $\underline{x}$ from the sentence $\underline{s}$, and by setting $\underline{b}*(\underline{x}) = \underline{T}$ for any other atomic sentence $\underline{x}$ from the language $\underline{L}$.

The concept of a valid sentence for $\underline{L}$ is also given in two forms:

A sentence of $\underline{L}$ is $\underline{b}$-valid iff it is nonfalse under every possible $\underline{b}$-model of the language $\underline{L}$.

A sentence of $\underline{L}$ is classically valid iff it is true under every possible $\underline{c}$-model of the language $\underline{L}$.

> $\underline{T}$ 3: All classically valid sentences are $\underline{b}$-valid.

Consider any sentence $\underline{s}$ that is not $\underline{b}$-valid. Let $\underline{b}$ be some $\underline{b}$-model such that $\underline{Vb}(\underline{s}) = \underline{F}$. Then by the construction of [T2], $\underline{Vb}*(\underline{s}) = \underline{F}$, hence $\underline{s}$ is not classically valid.

> $\underline{T}$ 4: All $\underline{b}$-valid sentences are classically valid.

Since the classical models are just the bivalent $\underline{b}$-models, and the classical valuations are just the bivalent $\underline{b}$-valuations, any sentence that is nonfalse under every $\underline{b}$-model is nonfalse under every $\underline{c}$-model. Since classical valuations are all bivalent, any such sentence will perforce be true in all classical models.

Thus we see that the $\underline{b}$-valid sentences of $\underline{L}$ exactly coincide with the classically valid sentences of $\underline{L}$; and we turn to logical consequence in the language $\underline{L}$. It will suffice here to define the consequence relation for the special case of a pair of sentences:

Q is a b-consequence of P iff the internal conditional $(P \supset Q)$ is b-valid, and is a c-consequence of P iff that internal conditional is c-valid.

> T 5: Neither truth nor nonfalsity is preserved under b-consequence.

It is readily verified that $(P \vee Q)$ is a b-consequence of P, and yet there are b-models which render P true and $(P \vee Q)$ nontrue: just take $Vb(Q) = I$. By contraposition, $\sim P$ is a b-consequence of $\sim(P \vee Q)$, and the same models render $\sim(P \vee Q)$ nonfalse and $\sim P$ false.

This indicates a slightly unorthodox feature of the BB-system; although b-consequence is fully classical (by [T3] and [T4]), no simple semantic characteristic of sentences appears to be preserved under it. The most that can be said in this regard apparently is:

> T 6: Logical validity is preserved under b-consequence; and Q is a b-consequence of P iff every b-model which renders P true, renders Q nonfalse.

Within the internal language L it is possible now to define a truth-operator 'w' to simulate a language having the first degree of semantic closure; let 'w' be given as the internal identity-connective having the matrix:

P	wP
T	T
F	F
I	I

This can be defined in various ways, for instance via double negation:

Definition 1: 'wP' $=_{df}$ '$\sim\sim P$'.

Now for any sentence P we can define a sentence expressing the proposition that P is true:

Definition 2: 'It is true that P' $=_{df}$ 'wP'.

and the equivalence-principle (Tarski's condition of adequacy) can be formulated schematically as $[wP \equiv P]$. Then:

> T 7: The equivalence-principle $[wP \equiv P]$ is valid in L.

By [T3] and [T4], b-validity and c-validity in L coincide, so no qualification is needed on further results concerning validity in L.

However, although each Tarski biconditional so formulated is $\underline{c}$-valid, that is, true in all classical valuations over $\underline{L}$, it is not thereby rendered true in all $\underline{b}$-valuations over $\underline{L}$. It is a simple matter to see then:

> $\underline{T}$ 8: For any $\underline{b}$-model of $\underline{L}$: All bivalent sentences have true Tarski biconditionals, and all other sentences have indeterminate Tarski biconditionals.

For, if $\underline{Vb}(\underline{P}) \neq \underline{I}$ then $\underline{Vb}(\underline{P}) = \underline{Vb}(w\underline{P})$ and $\underline{Vb}(w\underline{P} \equiv \underline{P}) = \underline{T}$; and if $\underline{Vb}(\underline{P}) = \underline{I}$ then $\underline{Vb}(\underline{P}) = \underline{Vb}(w\underline{P})$ and $\underline{Vb}(w\underline{P} \equiv \underline{P}) = \underline{I}$.

Let us say that a proposition is <u>expressible with respect to a b-model</u> iff some sentence grammatically constituted to express that proposition is bivalent under that model. Then:

> $\underline{T}$ 9: The language $\underline{L}$ has the first but not the second degree of semantic closure.

For any given $\underline{b}$-model $\underline{b}$ and any sentence $\underline{P}$, exactly one of the following cases obtains:

(i) $\underline{Vb}(\underline{P}) = \underline{T}$. Then the proposition that $\underline{P}$ is true is expressible by $w\underline{P}$.

(ii) $\underline{Vb}(\underline{P}) = \underline{F}$. Then the proposition that $\underline{P}$ is false is expressible by $w\sim\underline{P}$.

(iii) $\underline{Vb}(\underline{P}) = \underline{I}$. Then the proposition that $\underline{P}$ is indeterminate ($\sim w\underline{P}$ & $\sim w\sim\underline{P}$) is inexpressible, as is the proposition that $\underline{P}$ is not true ($\sim w\underline{P}$).

In spite of case (iii), the language $\underline{L}$ can be granted the first degree of semantic closure by interpreting the value $\underline{I}$ as the absence of a truth-value rather than the presence of a nonstandard truth-value. Strictly speaking, all that has been shown above is that certain propositions are expressible by way of the definition [D2], and that others are not so expressible. To establish more firmly the inexpressibility results it is requisite to show basically that the Bochvar-Frege horizontal is inexpressible in $\underline{L}$, i.e. that no connective having the following matrix is definable in $\underline{L}$:

P	hP
T	T
F	F
I	F

which is readily shown by way of the observation that any such connective would form, from a sentence to which it attaches, a necessarily bivalent sentence.

> T 10: No sentence of L is bivalent under all possible b-models.

There is one b-model that assigns the value I to every atomic sentence of L; its associated b-valuation in turn assigns the value I to every sentence of L, and establishes the result by one fell swoop.

The "Expanded" Language L+

The language L+ results from the language L by adjoining a single nonclassical connective, the Bochvar–Frege horizontal 'h' which we have just seen is inexpressible in L. Since the horizontal is a nonclassical connective, its attachment to any sentence will "seal off" the internal structure of that sentence so far as classical valuations of the language L+ are concerned; this calls for a distinction in L+ between atomic and classically elementary sentences:

> A sentence of L+ is <u>classically elementary</u> iff it is atomic or has the horizontal as its major connective.

Thus P, hP, h(P ⊃ (Q ⊃ R)) are all examples of classically elementary sentences. Any sentence of L+ now has two distinct logical factorizations: its <u>full factorization</u> down to atomic sentences, and its <u>classical factorization</u> down to its maximal classically elementary constituents. A few examples should render sufficiently clear the sense in which the classical constituents of any sentence of L+ are in general a subset of its full set of b-constituents:

Sentence	b-Constituents	Classical Constituents
h~P	h~P, ~P, P	h~P
~hP	~hP, hP, P	~hP, hP
(hQ ⊃ P)	(hQ ⊃ P), hQ, P, Q	(hQ ⊃ P), hQ, P

In particular, a sentence may have constituents that are classically elementary sentences but that are not classical constituents of that sentence, since they fall within the scope of some horizontal. These factors introduce the complication now that classical valuations of L+ no longer can be regarded as simply a subset of all valuations.

> A b-<u>model</u> of L+ is any function b assigning exactly one of the three values {T, F, I} to each atomic sentence of L+.
> A c-<u>model</u> of L+ is any function c assigning exactly one of the two values {T, F} to each classically elementary sentence of L+.

Each model now determines a valuation of the corresponding sort as before, with the sole difference that b-valuations now are reckoned in accordance with Bochvar's external matrix for the horizontal along with his internal matrices for the classical propositional connectives.

$\underline{T}$ 11: A sentence is bivalent under any $\underline{b}$-model $\underline{b}$ iff the associated valuation $\underline{Vb}$ is bivalent over each of the classical constituents of that sentence.

$\underline{T}$ 12: For any sentence $\underline{s}$ and any $\underline{b}$-model $\underline{b}$ such that $\underline{Vb}(\underline{s}) \in \{\underline{T}, \underline{F}\}$ there is a $\underline{c}$-model $\underline{b}^{**}$ such that $\underline{Vb}^{**}(\underline{s}) = \underline{Vb}(\underline{s})$.

Form $\underline{b}^{**}$ by setting $\underline{b}^{**}(\underline{x}) = \underline{Vb}(\underline{x})$ for each elementary classical constituent $\underline{x}$ from the sentence $\underline{s}$, and by setting $\underline{b}^{**}(\underline{x}) = \underline{T}$ for any other classically elementary sentence $\underline{x}$ from the language $\underline{L}$+.

Since $\underline{s}$ is bivalent by hypothesis, so are each of its classical constituents. Since the internal matrices reduce to the corresponding classical matrices in bivalent cases, the values $\underline{Vb}^{**}(\underline{s})$ and $\underline{Vb}(\underline{s})$ are bound to coincide.

Defining validity in the same way as for the language $\underline{L}$:

$\underline{T}$ 13: In the language $\underline{L}$+: All classically valid sentences are $\underline{b}$-valid.

Let $\underline{s}$ be any sentence that is not $\underline{b}$-valid; we must show that $\underline{s}$ is not $\underline{c}$-valid. By hypothesis, $\underline{s}$ is false under some $\underline{b}$-model. Let $\underline{b}$ be any such $\underline{b}$-model; then by [T12] we can form a $\underline{c}$-model $\underline{b}^{**}$ such that $\underline{Vb}^{**}(\underline{s}) = \underline{F}$; therefore $\underline{s}$ is not classically valid.

$\underline{T}$ 14: In the language $\underline{L}$+: The classically valid sentences are a proper subset of the $\underline{b}$-valid sentences.

For an example of a sentence that is $\underline{b}$-valid but not $\underline{c}$-valid, consider $(h{\sim}P \supset {\sim}hP)$. Truth-table analysis will verify that this sentence is $\underline{b}$-valid; that it is not classically valid is shown by any $\underline{c}$-model for which $\underline{c}(h{\sim}P) = \underline{c}(hP) = \underline{T}$.

The example of [T14] shows what has already been remarked, that some classical valuations of the language $\underline{L}$+ are not admissible within the BB-system, which takes account of a finer-than-classical propositional structure. The explanation within the present interpretation is that $\underline{L}$+ incorporates a portion of its own theory of truth (via the horizontal), along with its theory of classical molecular structure. We have already seen a sense in which even the internal language $\underline{L}$ can be construed as incorporating part of its own theory of truth, but so fragmentary a part as to leave unaltered the notion of validity. Consider now the extent to which $\underline{L}+$ can express its own semantics. Following Bochvar, semantical operators can be introduced by the defintions:

Definition 3:   'h$\underline{P}$'   = $_{df}$ 'It is true that $\underline{P}$';
                    'h$\sim\underline{P}$'   = $_{df}$ 'It is false that $\underline{P}$';
                    '$\sim$h$\underline{P}$&$\sim$h$\sim\underline{P}$'= $_{df}$ 'It is neither true nor false that $\underline{P}$'.

Abbreviating the English locutions, these definitions yield the matrices:

P	t$\underline{P}$	f$\underline{P}$	n$\underline{P}$
T	T	F	F
F	F	T	F
I	F	F	T

It may be noted that the operator '$\underline{w}$' is still available in the language $\underline{L}+$, yielding two alternative formulations of the equivalence-principle. The two operators '$\underline{t}$' and '$\underline{w}$' correlate neatly with the distinction between "safe" and "vulnerable" predications of truth, as exemplified by the distinction between quotational and nonquotational reference.[23] Suppose $\underline{P}$ is the sentence 'Snow is white', and it happens to be the one and only sentence written on a certain blackboard. Then t$\underline{P}$ and w$\underline{P}$ might express respectively the propositions expressed by:

> The sentence 'Snow is white' is true.
> The sentence on the board is true.

Within formalized languages the distinction coincides with designation by way of spelling (or formal quotation) as contrasted with designation by way of Gödel-numbers. The equivalence-principle can now be formulated schematically in either of two ways: [w$\underline{P}$ ≡ $\underline{P}$] as before, or else [t$\underline{P}$ ≡ $\underline{P}$]; but under the proposed interpretation, the latter is a more faithful rendering of Tarski's adherence to "structural-descriptive" names in his "Convention $\underline{T}$." In any case we have:

$\underline{T}$ 15: (a) The schema [w$\underline{P}$ ≡ $\underline{P}$] is both $\underline{b}$-valid and $\underline{c}$-valid in $\underline{L}+$.
          (b) The schema [t$\underline{P}$ ≡ $\underline{P}$] is $\underline{b}$-valid but not $\underline{c}$-valid in $\underline{L}+$.
          (c) The biconditional [w$\underline{P}$ ≡ $\underline{P}$] is true under any given $\underline{b}$-model of $\underline{L}+$ iff $\underline{P}$ is bivalent under that model, and is indeterminate otherwise.

23. See supra, note 19.

(d) The biconditional $[\underline{t}P \equiv \underline{P}]$ is true under any
given $\underline{b}$-model of $\underline{L}+$ iff $\underline{P}$ is bivalent under that
model, and is indeterminate otherwise.

Due to [T10], any proposition of the internal language $\underline{L}$ is expressible with respect to some $\underline{b}$-models and inexpressible with respect to others. The expanded language $\underline{L}+$ admits a stronger notion of expressibility:

A proposition is <u>absolutely</u> <u>expressible</u> in the language $\underline{L}+$ iff some sentence grammatically constituted to express that proposition is bivalent under all possible $\underline{b}$-models of the language $\underline{L}+$.

Now we have:

$\underline{T}$ 16: The language $\underline{L}+$ has the second degree of semantic closure.

For any sentence $\underline{P}$ of the language $\underline{L}+$, the sentence $\underline{t}P$ absolutely expresses the proposition that $\underline{P}$ is true, and the sentence $\sim \underline{t}P$ absolutely expresses the proposition that $\underline{P}$ is not true.

Defining consequence in the same way as for the language $\underline{L}$, [T13] and [T14] show that $\underline{b}$-consequence in $\underline{L}+$ is semiclassical. Indeed the notion of $\underline{b}$-consequence so defined has some further unorthodox features, as shown by:

$\underline{T}$ 17: (van Fraassen–Skyrms): In the language $\underline{L}+$, $\underline{b}$-consequence is nontransitive.
It can be verified that (i) and (ii) are $\underline{b}$-valid while (iii) is <u>not</u> $\underline{b}$-valid:

(i) $\sim \underline{hp} \supset (\underline{P} \equiv \underline{P})$
(ii) $(\underline{P} \equiv \underline{P}) \supset (\underline{hP} \text{ v } \underline{h{\sim}P})$
(iii) $\sim \underline{hP} \supset (\underline{hP} \text{ v } \underline{h{\sim}P})$

This result can be explained by considering the systematic import of the formulas involved. According to the definitions in [D3], the following rendering can be given of (i) through (iii):

(i) $\sim \underline{t}P \supset (\underline{P} \equiv \underline{P})$
(ii) $(\underline{P} \equiv \underline{P}) \supset \sim \underline{nP}$
(iii) $\sim \underline{t}P \supset \sim \underline{nP}$

The first two are vacuously $\underline{b}$-valid; indeed the first formula is even $\underline{c}$-valid. The third expresses the proposition that if $\underline{P}$ is nontrue then it is bivalent, which is patently not $\underline{b}$-valid. This result might possibly be rationalized by reflection on the mixed logical-semantic character of the language $\underline{L}+$. It might be interesting to work out a separation within $\underline{L}+$ of those sentences that are <u>logically</u>

valid from those sentences that are <u>analytic</u>, as follows. The first class would comprise those sentences that are <u>b</u>-valid in virtue of their logical structure alone (narrowly construed as excluding the horizontal), while the second class would comprise those sentences that are <u>b</u>-valid in virtue of their full semantic structure (more broadly construed as including the horizontal along with the classical connectives). The logically valid sentences would then be expected to coincide exactly with those which are classically valid. In particular, (i) but not (ii) above would come out logically valid under such a disentanglement, which might then be expected to yield a narrower consequence relation free from the irregularities of [T17].

Alternatively, the whole enterprise of trivalent semantics for semantically closed languages may well be brought into question. So far the differences between the supervaluation approach and the Bochvar–Buridan approach have been stressed, leaving in the background their shared assumption of a trivalent semantics.[24] It is quite possible however that a trivalent framework simply will not accommodate sharply enough Buridan's separation between correspondence conditions and presuppositions. The closest trivalent counterpart to satisfied correspondence conditions seem to be nonfalsity, and yet [T5] shows that nonfalsity is not preserved under <u>b</u>-consequence however construed, which is another symptom of some irregularity in this otherwise well-behaved and revealing logical theory. If conditions of correspondence and presuppositions are mutually independent conditions, then <u>four</u> rather than <u>three</u> values should be possible. Without pursuing the matter here, it may be remarked that initial studies with quadrivalent semantics indeed support this view and promise an alternative reconstruction of the radical logical theory outlined by Buridan.[25]

References

Bochvar, D. A.,   "On a Three-Valued Calculus and Its Application in the Analysis of the Paradoxes of the Extended Functional Calculus," <u>Matematicheskii Sbornik</u>, n.s. 4, 46 (1938), 287–308. [TVC]

Buridan, J.,   <u>Sophisms on Meaning and Truth</u>, ed. T. K. Scott, New York, Appleton-Century-Crofts, 1966. [SMT]

24. See supra, note 3.
25. See supra, note 12.

Fraassen, B. van,   "The Completeness of Free Logic," Zeitschr.
für math. Logik und Grundlagen d. Math., 12
(1966), 219–34. [CFL]

——,   "Singular Terms, Truth-Value Gaps, and
Free Logic," Journal of Philosophy, 63 (1966),
481–95. [STF]

——,   "Presupposition, Implication, and Self-Reference," Journal of Philosophy, 65 (1968),
136–52. [PIS]

——,   "Presuppositions, Supervaluations, and Free
Logic," in K. Lambert, ed., The Logical Way
of Doing Things, New Haven, Yale University
Press, 1969. [PSF]

——,   "Truth and Paradoxical Consequences," this
volume. [TPC]

Frege, G.,   The Basic Laws of Arithmetic, ed. M. Furth,
Berkeley and Los Angeles, University of California Press, 1964. [BL]

Herzberger, H. G., and Katz, J. J., "The Concept of Truth in Natural
Languages," manuscript, Boston, 1966–67.
[CTNL]

Kleene, S. C.,   Introduction to Metamathematics, New York,

Lewis, D. K.,   Von Nostrand 1952. [IM] "Counterpart Theory
and Quantified Modal Logic," Journal of Philosophy, 65 (1968), 113–26. [CT]

Matheson, G.,   "The Semantics of Singular Terms," Journal
of Symbolic Logic, 27 (1962), 439–66. [SST]

McCall, S.,   "Temporal Flux," American Philosophical
Quarterly, 3 (1966), 270–81. [TF]

Prior, A.,   Past, Present and Future, Oxford, Clarendon
Press, 1967. [PPF]

Skyrms, B.,   "Return of the Liar: Three-Valued Logic and
the Concept of Truth," mimeo. 1967, forthcoming in American Philosophical Quarterly. [RL]

——,   "Supervaluations: Identity, Existence, and Individual Concepts," Journal of Philosophy, 65
(1968), 477–82. [S]

Smiley, T.,   "Sense Without Denotation," Analysis, 2 (1960),
125–35. [SWD]

Smullyan, R.,   "Languages in Which Self-Reference is Possible," Journal of Symbolic Logic, 22 (1959),
55–67. [LSRP]

——,   Theory of Formal Systems, Princeton, Princeton University Press, 1961. [TFS]

Tarski, A.,   "The Semantic Conception of Truth," Philosophy
and Phenomenological Research, 4 (1944). [SCT]

Some Remarks Prompted by van Fraassen's Paper

by John T. Kearns

I wish to argue that van Fraassen's results support one solution
to one of the philosophical problems of self-reference. I am concerned with the results obtained in his earlier paper, "Presupposition, Implication, and Self-Reference" (The Journal of Philosophy,
65 [1968]), as well as those presented in this volume. The problem
is that of dealing with, or understanding, the paradoxical consequences of certain self-referential sentences. These sentences
can be formulated in ordinary language, and they pose a problem
with respect to ordinary language,[1] or our ordinary conceptual
framework. The trouble-making sentences seem to be legitimately formed from significant expressions. For there is nothing initially outrageous about self-reference. And the affirmation and
denial of truth or falsity seem to be perfectly in order. But if
these sentences are uncritically accepted, they generate contradictory consequences. The philosophical task I am undertaking is
to understand just what is wrong: to uncover a mistaken belief or
an unrecognized confusion.

Let me indicate what I mean by ordinary language and our ordinary conceptual framework. (I am interested only in ordinary
language assertions, both possible and actual—as opposed to questions, commands, and the rest.) Ordinary language is the language
people actually use, but it is not simply the language of ordinary
people. Ordinary language in my sense includes technical terms,
as well as certain associated rules, principles, and techniques. I
speak of our ordinary conceptual framework when I wish to make
claims that are more general than claims about ordinary English;
the "same" conceptual framework can be expressed by more than
one language.[2]

1. I don't mean to suggest that the self-referring sentences make
difficulties for nonphilosophers who use ordinary language. These sentences cause trouble for those of us who want to understand ordinary
language, or our ordinary conceptual framework.

2. Although a conceptual framework is general with respect to languages, I will regard it as existing in time. For a conceptual framework
can be changed, as by the introduction of new concepts. This is not the
most common way of talking about the conceptual order, but it seems to
me to be the most adequate one.

Van Fraassen's discussion is not directed to ordinary language or our ordinary conceptual framework. He is concerned with formal languages and with certain relations between sentences in such languages. But his results can be brought to bear on my problem, and he indicates that this was one of his goals. However, the use I wish to make of them is different from the one he suggests. For I think that van Fraassen has assimilated relations between propositions to relations between sentences in a confusing way. By distinguishing these two kinds of relations, we can achieve a clearer understanding of what his results establish.

To make good my claim about van Fraassen's assimilation, I will begin by discussing presupposition, as it has been treated by Strawson. For van Fraassen appears to regard his own logical results as illustrating or illuminating, as well as developing the consequences of, Strawson's position. Instead of confronting Strawson's position head-on, I will approach it via the consideration of some of Frege's views. For Strawson's account of presupposition, at least existential presupposition, is a modified version of Frege's account, and Frege's arguments are superior to Strawson's. I accept neither Frege's reasons nor his account of presupposition, but I recognize that reasons like his are at least the right sort of reasons to support such an account.

Frege introduced the concept of existential presupposition in discussing singular terms that fail to designate real individuals (I shall call such terms <u>empty</u> terms). The most obvious singular terms of this sort are (some) definite descriptions, like 'the king of France in 1960'. But Frege also recognized empty proper names, like 'Pegasus'. It is Frege's view that, outside of a fictional situation, when a singular term is used to refer, the existence of a referent is presupposed. If this presupposition fails, then the sentence that contains the singular term is neither true nor false.

Frege's view about presupposition must be understood in relation to his view that sentences (of the sort that can be asserted) are singular terms. For Frege, a singular term has a sense and (possibly) a reference. The sense of a sentence is a proposition. (Frege's terminology was different, but the distinction he made between a sentence and its sense is clearly the same as that currently drawn between a sentence and the proposition it expresses.) The reference of a sentence is rather peculiar, for Frege recognized two objects, the True and the False, that are named by sentences. It is characteristic of natural languages that some of their singular terms, such as 'Pegasus' and 'the king of France in 1960', have no reference. A general principle concerning complex singular terms (singular terms that contain other singular terms as parts) is that a complex singular term is empty if one of its component singular terms is empty (e.g. 'the owner of Pegasus'). But a sentence is a complex singular term; so if it contains an empty component, it must also be empty. An empty sentence is one that is neither true nor false.

For Frege, a sentence whose presupposition fails is perfectly intelligible, and it expresses a proposition; but this sentence is neither true nor false. Frege's view here is an incidental consequence of his view that sentences are names, and that they name the True and the False. Strawson has taken over Frege's claim that sentences containing referring terms are sentences with (existential) presuppositions, and that a sentence whose presupposition fails is neither true nor false. But he has abandoned the philosophical underpinning of Frege's view, and this leaves him with nothing to rely on except ordinary language, which is less than conclusive on this point.

If Frege's strange objects, the True and the False, are given up, there no longer seems to be a good reason for saying that a sentence whose existential presupposition fails is neither true nor false. For what matters is not whether ordinary people speaking ordinarily would say that such a sentence is false. What matters is what we choose to call such sentences. Ordinary language does not consist only of expressions, with rules for their use; it also includes resources which enable us to introduce new expressions or to give a new sense to existing expressions. The distinction between significant sentences (proposition-expressing sentences) that are true and those that are not is a distinction which can be, and frequently has been, marked with the words 'true' and 'false'. If this does not accord with the ordinary man's use of 'false' then we are using the term in a technical way. But there are no paradoxical consequences of a decision to use 'false' so that a sentence whose existential presupposition fails is false.[3]

My remarks about Frege's account of existential presupposition should not be taken as a denial that there is such a relation as presupposition. This relation is genuine and important. The sentence (or the proposition it expresses)

---

3. Frege seems to have recognized that, ontological considerations aside, there is something arbitrary about denying the predicate 'is false' to sentences containing empty names. For in constructing his "ideal" language, Frege provided a reference for terms we would ordinarily regard as empty, so that the ideal language counterparts of neither-true-nor-false sentences turn out false.

(1) The king of France in 1960 was bald

presupposes

(2) There was a king of France in 1960.

But this is presupposition in something like the ordinary sense. It is quite reasonable to say that both (1) and (2) are false though they are false for different reasons. This relation of presupposition is a relation between significant sentences — a propositional relation. We can recognize and investigate this sort of presupposition without for a moment countenancing truth-value gaps.

Strawson and van Fraassen have given accounts (definitions) of presupposition that are more general than existential presupposition. But such presupposition includes two very different kinds of relations. The relation between significant sentences, of which the leading instance is existential presupposition, has normally been regarded as the relation that makes presupposition worth talking about. But this presupposition does not require a middle between truth and falsity. The second sort of presupposition is a relation such that the truth of the presupposition is a requirement for significance. An example might be the sentence

(3) α is green

which (it is claimed) presupposes something like

(4) α is a physical object.

If (4) is not true, then (3) is not significant. Such a relation is not a propositional relation at all. Once this kind of presupposition is recognized, we find that every sentence has innumerable presuppositions. Indeed, any string of words can be said to presuppose that its components are meaningful and that they are significantly arranged. (Perhaps the preceding remark should be confined to those strings satisfying some criterion of grammaticalness.) It may be that the second sort of presupposition is also important. Van Fraassen has shown that it can be given an extremely elegant formal treatment. But an abstract treatment of this presupposition does not seem to shed much light on the particular instances of the relation that have an independent interest for us.

What I have said so far may suggest that I am unwilling to recognize grammatical sentences that do not express propositions, that I will not stand for truth-value gaps. This is not the case. I wish to maintain that the paradoxical sentences fail to express propositions, and I will use van Fraassen's results in explaining their failure. But I do not think the paradoxical sentences can helpfully

be viewed as exemplifying a special sort of presupposition failure.[4]

In order to understand van Fraassen's results and to apply
them toward a solution to the problem I am considering, we can
consider a very simple sort of formal language. This can be a
language that contains the standard truth-functional connectives,
predicates, and singular terms. I will suppose that this language
has a definite interpretation, and that this interpretation is made
in terms of our ordinary conceptual framework—that the significance of the terms used is explained by using ordinary language
expressions. It is not required that there be a simple translation
of each formal language schema or sentence into ordinary language
but only that we can use ordinary language to explain how to understand and use the expressions of the formal language. A formal
language interpreted in this way furnishes, in effect, a canonical
notation for saying what we want to say. Because it is merely a
canonical notation, the study of such a formal language can be directly relevant to philosophical problems about our ordinary conceptual framework. This way of interpreting and using a formal
language is to be contrasted with the approach in which the schemata are presented and results obtained about various interpretations. Such results can be useful in establishing the consistency
of some view, but they are not automatically relevant to problems
concerning our ordinary conceptual framework.

It should already be clear that van Fraassen's treatment of
necessitation and supervaluation, which is central to his paper,
is not relevant to my discussion. Necessitation is the relation between sentences that enables us to determine that the self-referential sentences which concern us would lead to contradictions if
they expressed propositions. (Since they don't express propositions, these sentences don't imply anything.) And supervaluations
provide a way to give a special status to sentences (and formulas)
valid in a two-valued scheme, even when components of these sentences fail to be true or false. But we do not need supervaluations
for dealing with significant sentences whose presuppositions fail;
I have decided to call them _false_. And we can understand the failure of the paradoxical sentences to express propositions without
exploring necessitation and supervaluation.

---

4. It is true that, in the sense defined by van Fraassen, the paradoxical sentences have presuppositions that are not true. So will any
sentence that does not express a proposition. But van Fraassen's analysis does not succeed in reducing these problem sentences to some well-
understood situation.

To properly understand the paradoxical sentences, I think we should consider vague expressions, or concepts. By a vague expression I mean one for which the criteria are inadequate for determining whether it is applicable in every case. A vague expression is one for which there are borderline cases. Suppose a predicate 'R' (which might be used to say that an individual is red) is vague, and that a is an individual which is a borderline case for 'R'. When this happens, it seems to me to be correct to say that the sentence

(5) R(a)

is neither true nor false. Similarly, the sentence

(6) ~R(a)

is neither true nor false. It might be objected that to say that (6) is neither true nor false is to interpret '~' as a rather limited negation (a choice-negation); that there is another negation, say '¬', so that

(7) ¬ R(a)

is true. But (6) is the proper denial of (5); to deny a sentence is not to deny that it has a truth-value. The '¬' in (7) can only be understood as a predicate whose argument is the sentence (5).[5]

In a formal language, as in ordinary language, we can allow ourselves to talk about sentences (sentence types), and to distinguish those sentences that are true, those that are false, and those that are neither. Let us use 'T' and 'F' to say that a sentence is true or is false. In order to use these predicates for talking about sentences, we can use some kind of quoting device, or introduce names for sentences (sentence types). If quoting is used it must be sentential quoting as opposed to what I shall call propositional quoting. Sentential quoting is sometimes accomplished in ordinary language by using single quotes; it is used to focus on the sign-design exemplified (although allowance must be made for such things

---

5. If one thinks of connectives merely as functional expressions whose significance is determined by a three-valued matrix, it is easy to overlook the distinction between '~' and '¬'. But it is one thing to characterize a function in terms of its arguments and values, and another to realize (or express) the function with the resources of language. The ordinary connectives (~, v, ⊃, etc.) are propositional connectives, and their use does not involve the mention of the sentences they join. Use of a connective that yields a true or a false sentence when its components are neither true nor false requires that we mention the sentences it connects.

as different type styles). Propositional quoting is used to focus on the meaningful expression exemplified;[6] the 'that' in a that-clause often serves for propositional quoting. Propositional quoting can be properly used only with proposition-expressing sentences. In the example above, if we suppose that we can effectively determine that $\underline{a}$ is a borderline case for 'R' (which need not be the case), we can say that both

$$\sim T('R(\underline{a})'), \ \sim F('R(\underline{a})')$$

are true. In future examples, these single quotes will be built into the parentheses accompanying 'T', 'F'—as

$$\sim T(R(\underline{a})), \ \sim F(R(\underline{a})).[7]$$

Now consider what happens with self-referential sentences. It is clear that not all of these sentences give trouble. For if 'G' is a predicate which means is grammatical, and α is the sentence

$$G(\alpha),$$

then α is true: $T(\alpha)$. But if β is the sentence

$$F(\beta),$$

then β gives trouble. We must say that β is neither true nor false. But we cannot say this by writing

$$\sim T(\beta) \ \& \sim F(\beta).$$

For if '$\sim F(\beta)$' is true then β is false, which is impossible. In an analogous fashion, the Strengthened Liar sentence γ:

$$\sim T(\gamma)$$

raises difficulties. For neither of

$$T(\gamma), \ \sim T(\gamma)$$

is either true or false. What I think this shows is that the predicates 'F' and 'T' (and the concepts of falsity and truth) are vague, and that β and γ are borderline cases for these predicates.

---

6. Propositional quoting is clearly a special case of a quoting that can be used with (significant) expressions of any length. The general distinction I have in mind is that found in many articles by Sellars. For he frequently uses (ordinary) quotes for attending to sign-designs and dot-quotes for focusing on the roles of the quoted expressions.

7. Because of the distinction between sentential and propositional quoting, it is incorrect to read

$$T(\underline{R}(\underline{a}))$$

as "it is true that $\underline{R}(\underline{a})$." Instead it should be "Sentence '$\underline{R}(\underline{a})$' is true."

If we iterate the predicates 'T' and 'F' with or without negation, we can form sentences about β and γ that are true or false. For example, it seems reasonable to say that

$$\sim T(\sim T(\sim T(\gamma))), \sim F(\sim T(\sim T(\gamma)))$$

are true. And this suggests a strategy for making our vague concepts more precise (textbook discussions of definition commonly indicate that this is an important use for definitions). For we could introduce a stronger predicate 'T_1' which is generated from 'T' and is such that

$$\sim T_1(\gamma)$$

is true. But with this new predicate we can form new and "stronger" paradoxical sentences. For van Fraassen has shown that no matter how often we iterate our original predicates (and no matter what additional predicates we introduce) we can never reach a point (or level) where all sentences are true or false. In fact, we can form sentences such that no amount of iteration will ever produce a sentence that is true or false.

These results are perplexing because it initially seemed that we could "solve" the paradoxes by admitting that some sentences are neither true nor false and placing the paradoxical sentences in that category. But when we provide ourselves with the resources for saying that sentences are true or false, we also provide ourselves with the resources for constructing paradoxical sentences that contain the very predicates we use for attributing truth and falsity. In his earlier paper, van Fraassen concluded that "To be presuppositionless may be a regulative ideal in philosophy, but it is not an achievable end." ("Presupposition, Implication, and Self-Reference," p. 150.) I find this misleading, for the 'presupposition' in the title does not carry anything like its normal sense, which is the sense intended by someone making such a claim. The reason we cannot introduce a global predicate 'is true', or reach a level where there are only true and false sentences, is that our concepts of truth and falsity are vague. It is not sufficient to recognize their vagueness by allowing for sentences that are neither true nor false. For when a concept is vague, there is no reason to expect its borderline area to be sharply delineated. What van Fraassen's results show is not simply that our concepts of truth and falsity are vague, but that they are incorrigibly vague.

Perhaps I should indicate why I regard my explanation of the paradoxical sentences in terms of vagueness as a different sort of explanation, and a better one, than that given by van Fraassen.[8]

---

8. Of course, one reason may be because it is my explanation.

For van Fraassen has justified the claim that the paradoxical sentences fail because their presuppositions are contradictory (in the sense of 'presupposition' he has defined). But I think of an explanation of or a solution to a problem as its reduction to something with which we are familiar. Vagueness is a characteristic of language that has been recognized and discussed for some time. An explanation in terms of vagueness satisfies my criterion. In addition, I believe that by relating vagueness to the paradoxical sentences, I have shed new light on these sentences. The relation of presupposition on which significance depends is not an old familiar relation. Even disregarding this, the introduction of the concept of such presupposition sheds no particular light on the paradoxes. To say that the paradoxical sentences have contradictory presuppositions is not news; it is just another way of saying that their acceptance would lead to contradictions.

There is one rather serious difficulty about my way of understanding the paradoxes of self-reference. For I have said that certain sentences which appear to deny that they possess a characteristic do not in fact possess that characteristic. But the sentences in question fail to be true or false while my sentences are alleged to be true. Why is it that my sentences are not in the same boat with the failing sentences?

So long as we restrict ourselves to sentences in different languages, my procedure might be justified by the object language–metalanguage distinction. For my predicate 'is true' is not a predicate of the formal language. Of course, I have used the predicate 'is true' to explain the significance of 'T' in the formal language, but I might still manage to make it out that when I use the predicate 'is true' to talk about sentences in a different language, the claims I make about sentences in that language are not claims that can be made with sentences in that language. But the formal language has been used to shed light on ordinary language and our ordinary conceptual framework. So the object language–metalanguage distinction merely postpones the difficulty. For now what is wanted is a plausible account of sentence A:

(A) Sentence A is not true.

This sentence belongs to ordinary language, which seems to be the ultimate metalanguage. To deal with sentence A in the manner of the preceding section, I should say that A is neither true nor false. But in order to get away with saying this, I must show that when I say that A is not true I am saying something different from what A seems to be saying about itself.

My proposal for resolving this difficulty does not seem to me entirely satisfactory, but I am becoming convinced that it is correct. To understand it, consider once more the formal language in which γ is

$$\sim T(\gamma).$$

In connection with γ, I pointed out that it is possible to introduce a strengthened predicate 'T_1' for truth so that

$$\sim T_1(\gamma)$$

is true. Once such a predicate is introduced, new possibilities for self-reference are available. But then a new predicate can be introduced, and so on. This is how I propose to understand the situation in ordinary language. But in ordinary language, we normally would not introduce a new predicate. Instead, the same predicate is used to express a new concept. So that when I say that sentence A is not true, I am expressing a stronger concept of truth than does the predicate in sentence A. And there is no end to these concepts of truth; for any concept we can introduce a stronger one. In fact there is no such thing as the concept of truth (nor is there a strongest concept of truth). Our conceptual framework is essentially open-ended (this is a more positive way of putting it than saying that our conceptual framework is essentially incomplete). The conceptual framework can always be extended with new concepts, including new concepts of truth.

There is some similarity between this view and theories of types or of language levels. But according to my view, neither ordinary language nor our ordinary conceptual framework is neatly stratified into types or levels. And self-reference is not illicit. We can talk about the expressions in a language in that same language; we can talk about the very expressions we are using. Theories of types or language levels are approximations to the view I am proposing. But such theories would have us refrain from saying things that can very well be said.

In conclusion I want to consider what it means to say that I have solved the problem I originally proposed. My solution is that any concept of truth that is not arbitrarily restricted will prove incorrigibly vague, and that our ordinary conceptual framework is essentially open. The failure of attempts to attribute or deny truth to a certain sentence can be accounted for if we introduce a new concept of truth. Such an introduction is very natural, for we seem to understand the concept without explicit recognition that it is new.

It may help if I contrast what I have been doing with an attempt to devise a technique for coping with the paradoxes. What I have in mind is a technique that keeps the paradoxes from arising. Such a technique is only appropriate when we are considering an artificial language. In formal languages there can be various devices for heading off paradoxes. One such device is to base the language on a theory of types. Skyrms and Martin have explored others.

When the paradoxes are considered with respect to ordinary language, it makes little sense to speak of introducing a technique for eliminating them. Ordinary language is not a language that is being set up. It is already there, and I am trying to understand what is responsible for the paradoxes. However, it can be argued that a technique used in a formal language corresponds to certain principles that govern the use of ordinary language. I believe Russell felt this way about the theory of types. I have already indicated reasons for not accepting such a theory, so let us briefly consider the accounts of Skyrms and Martin. Initially I think that there is considerable plausibility to Skyrms' approach; at least, what he is trying to do is perfectly reasonable. For he wants to have the paradoxical sentences fail to be either true or false, and he wants to allow us to say this. But his approach suggests no principles that can plausibly be said to govern ordinary speech. He has divided the sentences in his language into two groups and devised rules that never take one from sentences in the preferred group to a sentence in the other. But these rules are in no sense "natural." And while there is some analogy between his predicate 'T', as interpreted, and our predicate 'is true', the analogy breaks down just at the point that most concerns us, the self-referring sentences.

Martin, in his account, has adopted a device that is suggested by our ordinary language. We do not, for instance, attribute colors to such things as sounds; nor do we utter sentences like 'That sound was not red.' If we asked someone if a certain sound was red, he would probably not say no. Instead, he would probably give us a bewildered look. The trouble with Martin's account is that for ordinary, nonsemantical predicates, or concepts, there is nothing to prevent us from stipulating that they shall be used so that they can be (truly) denied of more things than they ordinarily would. We obtain no contradictory results if we agree to say that sounds are not red. The only concepts for which we cannot relax the ranges of applicability are certain semantical ones. But this strongly suggests that his treatment is ad hoc; there is something special about the concept of truth which he has not explained. Another shortcoming is that, in his language, we are not allowed to use a predicate to designate those sentences that fail to be true, although we can, in effect, say this of a sentence. In Martin's language, as in languages based on a theory of types, we find restrictions that are readily intelligible and that block contradictions. But neither sort of restriction enables us to account for the paradoxical character of the paradoxes, because neither sort of restriction must inevitably characterize significant speech.

My way of accounting for the paradoxes is to understand what has gone wrong, not to devise methods for banishing them. But in a sense my account does eliminate the paradoxes. For I do not believe that two contradictory sentences are both true, nor do I believe that in employing ordinary language I am committed to accepting a contradiction. The paradoxes result from a mistaken belief that there is, or can be, a global predicate 'is true' or a global concept of truth. It is because this belief initially seems to be reasonable that the paradoxes are puzzling. My solution eliminates the paradox but not the puzzle.

Rejoinder: On a Kantian Conception of Language

by Bas C. van Fraassen

Both Kearns and Herzberger[1] have, in their stimulating and per-
spicacious comments, directed themselves mainly to the conception of the structure of language that underlies my analysis of the
paradoxes, rather than to the details of that analysis. And each
has explored a significant alternative, based on rival intuitions
concerning language. In answer I shall try to develop my own conception in some more detail, with special attention to the questions they have forced me to confront.

Ordinary and Natural Language

Kearns argues that the paradoxes of self-reference must be dealt
with where they are encountered, namely in ordinary language.
But he hastens to explain the sense in which he uses "ordinary language": in his sense, it "is the language that people actually use,
but it is not simply the language of ordinary people." In ordinary
language he includes technical jargon developed for special purposes, and with it he associates certain rules, principles, and techniques. And sometimes he refers rather to "our ordinary conceptual framework," embodied in English, but not solely in English. In
addition, he is wont to point out that we stay within ordinary language, in his sense, when we introduce new means of expression—
as when he comments on Martin's approach that there is nothing to
prevent us from agreeing henceforth to say that red truly does not
apply to sounds.

   Now I would like to draw a distinction here between ordinary
language and natural language. Mankind always has spoken and always will speak the latter; it consists in the resources we have for
saying what we want to say. The former is the "part" of those resources that we have realized, that are actually at our disposal
now, and that are equally at the disposal of any native (or sufficiently educated nonnative) speaker. I humbly propose that the philosophers in the tradition familiarly known as "ordinary language philosophy" direct[ed] themselves to what I call ordinary language,

---

1. My reasons for taking up the second commentary first are purely
didactic.

and that Kearns and I alike are addressing ourselves to natural language.

Vagueness and Presuppositions

Kearns agrees that paradoxical sentences are neither true nor false, but argues that to be adequate, a solution to the paradoxes must show _why_ they are neither true nor false. Rejecting my attempt to explain these truth-value gaps via the notion of presupposition,[2] he offers an account in terms of vagueness. Some predicates are vague, i.e. have "borderline cases," and when a vague predicate is applied to one of its borderline cases, the result is neither true nor false. The paradoxes show that "is true" is vague, and indeed that it is _demonstrably_ and _incorrigibly_ vague. In this it differs from the ordinary cases that are corrigible: no contradiction arises from the decision henceforth to deny redness of the theory of relativity, but a contradiction would result from denying truth of the Strengthened Liar.

In answer I should like to offer a presuppositional analysis of vagueness. In our language we have criteria for the application of predicates — using the term 'application' to cover both the assertion and the denial of a given predicate of a given term.[3] Now the main presupposition of a sentence of form _Fb_ is that some criterion of application of the predicate _F_ be satisfied by the term _b_. (It would not hurt my account to assume that this is in fact the only kind of presupposition there is.[4]) A borderline case for _F_ is a case in which none of these criteria are satisfied; _F_ is vague if it has

2. Kearns also argues that Strawson was not faithful to the Fregean account of presuppositions, and that I, at least, have assimilated various other semantic relations to that of presupposition. In my view, his emphasis on Frege's account leads him to assimilate all presuppositions to existential presuppositions. In any case, my definition of presupposition is that explicitly given by Strawson in his reply to Sellars (see the references in [PRIM]). (Bracketed abbreviations refer to references in the paper by van Fraassen, pp. 13–23, above.)

3. It might be more natural to say that the object referred to as _b_ satisfies or does not satisfy the criteria; but we must not forget our brothers the nonexistents: "The king of France," rather than the king of France, fails to satisfy the relevant criteria once they are phrased in a philosophically perspicuous idiom.

4. This brings my account very close also to Martin's, for _b_ is not a borderline case for _F_ in the above sense if and only if the referent of _b_ is in the range of application of _F_, if I understand that correctly (see Robert L. Martin, "A Category Solution to the Liar" in this volume).

borderline cases. And truth demonstrably and incorrigibly admits of borderline cases.

This assertion of incorrigibility, however, must be qualified; the truth-value gaps could be filled if we give up certain basic principles, such as the soundness of classical logic, or the mutual necessitation of a sentence and the statement that this sentence is true. In more mundane cases, truth-value gaps can be filled by introducing new criteria of application to cover the hitherto unforeseen cases. (And judges presumably are called upon to do this; for example, in reaching a decision on whether burning a draftcard counts as symbolic speech.) But the point is that, as it stands, the language is _not_ such that facts and extant conventions determine the truth-value of all sentences. The language has, at any stage of its evolution, a certain incompleteness of means of expression, any given aspect of which may be remedied in its further evolution. This does not imply, of course, that this incompleteness will ever be entirely removed; the paradoxes lead to the conclusion that without violence to our most basic principles this could never be so.

Antinomies, Cosmic and Semantic

I should like at this point to suggest an analogy: that the semantic paradoxes play the role in our philosophy of language played by the Antinomies in the development of Kant's philosophy of the physical world.[5] Consider the question faced by Kant: Is the world a finite or an infinite totality? The natural conception of the world appears to entail that one of these must be the case—but note that the question presupposes that the world is a totality, a determinate whole. Kant's answer was that this presupposition is mistaken, that the world exists as an ever incomplete construction, as a task to be completed and not as a completed task. This general solution carries over to more specific questions concerning objects and events in the world. For example, the natural standpoint involves the assumption that either some state of the world is the first, or the sequence of past states is infinite. But, Kant argued, the supposition that for some such state X, 'X is the first' is true, leads to absurdity, as does the supposition that for all such states X, 'X is the first' is false. But once the presupposition that there

5. Which has often been said to be analogous to the role played by the set-theoretical paradoxes in the development of Brouwer's philosophy of mathematics, in just the way that I shall suggest here. This is not to be read as an endorsement of Kant's treatment of the Antinomies, nor of Brouwer's Intuitionism, I hasten to add.

is a determinate sequence of world-states comprising world history as a completed whole is given up, absurdity is avoided.

We must note that the derivations involved appeal to principles of causality (of states as determined or conditioned by previous states), which are not so dearly cherished by us as they were by Kant. But in the case of language we find our most cherished principles threatened by antinomies: the semantic paradoxes. Counsel to relinquish these principles is not easily followed here; and in this I believe we are in a better position than Kant. The situation is this: in the natural standpoint, we think of our language as a determinate structure, each sentence true or false, and semantically closed—whatever can be said, can be said in our language. But when this is pushed beyond the bounds of everyday sense, antinomies arise. (Not, however, within those bounds, which is why we can ordinarily sidestep these issues.) My skeptical solution is that this conception of language is mistaken.

Returning momentarily to Kant: if not an object, a determinate whole, a totality—what then is the world? There are of course different construals of his answer, and since the present purpose is didactic rather than historical, I shall give the one that pleases me. We have experience of objects and events, and in this experience these objects and events are given as part of the world. Any phenomenologically correct description of experience must certainly imply this: that a house front appears to me as the front of a house, not as a façade, and the street before me appears as leading to further determinate earthly structures. But what is the status of this part of the world outside my experience? According to Kant, the world is constituted in my experience, so that this "outer" part has the status of something yet to be constituted. But this constitution is according to definite rules—and, knowing these rules, we know the general structure of the world not yet constituted in experience. But what is real here are those rules; they do not determine the further construction uniquely, and what they leave indeterminate is at this point neither thus nor so.[6]

---

6. In Brouwer we find an exactly similar conception of mathematical objects. Consider the real number which is the infinite decimal $r = 3.1 \ldots$, where the third and succeeding digits are to be determined by the tossing of a die. We know that $3.1 < r < 3.17$, because the other digits will lie strictly between zero and seven. But $r < 3.16$ can be neither asserted nor denied at this point. What is real here is the rule of construction alone; and this rule does not determine the truth-value of $r < 3.16$.

Similarly, I want to argue that language is wholly determinate with respect to all normal contexts: in all familiar cases objective facts and linguistic conventions together determine the truth-value of each statement. In addition the structure of our language (constituted in my view by our linguistic commitments[7]—but that is not essential here) determines in a general way how our criteria of application may be extended, as we go on, to cover borderline cases and unforeseen situations. But all that is _real_ about the domain of sense yet to be appropriated are our (largely implicit) rules for going on. The rules for going on were on Kant's view entirely classical; the traditional metaphysics had only been mistaken by thinking of the rules as having been entirely implemented already, and of the world as a completed task existing independent of human sensibilities. Analogously, the rules for going on in language are on my view entirely classical; but the paradoxes show that we _cannot_ think of the extension as having been completed.

Ideal Extensions

Any philosophical position must answer to the demand that the phenomena be saved. In the pre-Critical stage, specifically in his Inaugural Dissertation, Kant had developed an explicit theory of the structure of the physical world (the general _form_ which the physical world must have) as conceived in the physical cosmology of his age. There is simply no denying that the scientific world picture is of the world as a determinate whole, and Kant had to reckon with this. His response is to accept the general form delineated in the dissertation as that determined by the Categories, the rules for the constitution of the world in experience. Each determinate structure agreeing with experience so far and embeddable in that general form is an ideal extension of what is determinately the case—and _physical_ _cosmology_ _is_ _the_ _theory_ _of_ _these_ _ideal_ _extensions._ This system of the world is perfectly successful in all its applications within the realm of experience—the antinomies arise only when its principles are not applied solely within the safe realm of the empirically given. Reasoning on subjects _within_ the world may always proceed on the assumptions prescribed by the regulative ideal of a unified science of the entire physical world. But reasoning _about_ the world cannot proceed along these lines without leading to absurdity.

We are similarly faced with a highly successful theory concerning valid reasoning, which always proceeds within the picture

---

7. See my "Meaning Relations among Predicates," _Nous_ 1 (1967), 161–79; failures of bivalence are not taken into account there, but can be handled along the lines of [PRUF].

of language as determinate in all respects: every sentence true or false, and the familiar rules of logic governing all possible described circumstances. Here we must save the phenomena. Classical logic must remain sound within its proper domain, and we must show why. And here my view, made explicit in several places now, is that classical logic is the theory of the ideal extensions of the valuations that exactly reflect what is the case. All classically valid arguments formulable within the language are sound. But the arguments about arguments whose correctness was tested by noting that they led from classically valid arguments to classically valid arguments lead to paradoxes when applied outside their proper realm. To put it yet another way: any statement is to be conceived of as true or false within the purely logical appraisal of arguments within the language. This will never lead us wrong, although it is clearly not adequate unto the full complexity of semantic connections within our language. But uncritically applied, this regulative ideal for mundane argument leads to a mistaken conception of natural language as entirely determinate.

Less metaphorically, the point is of course that the mobilization of human linguistic resources in the course of actual history is only one of the set of possible—but mutually incompatible—realizations of these resources. I can introduce a way of expressing nontruth within my language (with a new truth-predicate); I can also introduce new paradoxes destroying those means of expression; but I cannot have both at once.

By now I have repeated myself to some extent; and it is also time to emphasize that the analogy to Kant is only meant as one possible way to view the use of supervaluations. It is time perhaps to turn to the misgivings Herzberger voiced with respect to this device. He agrees at least to some extent that classical logic should be retained as far as possible,[8] but argues that matrices rather than supervaluations provide the correct device. Specifically he says that my $\equiv$ is not really material equivalence, because $(p \equiv q)$ may not be true although both p and q are neither true nor false, and thereby materially equivalent (Herzberger, "Truth and Modality in Semantically Closed Languages," p. 29). Now I would quite agree with the quoted inference if I thought of truth-value gaps in the way he does. For he treats sentences that are neither

---

8. With respect to his use of the 'external matrices' for this purpose it should be pointed out that the set of 'secure sentences' (the theorems of the corresponding logic) is not closed under the classical consequence relation: $A v \sim A$, $A \equiv h(A)$, and $(\sim A) \equiv h(\sim A)$, are secure, but not $h(A) v h(\sim A)$.

true nor false as having a third value. Hence within his framework, the inference in question amounts to: $T \neq v(p) \neq F$ and $T \neq v(q) \neq F$, hence $v(p) = v(q)$, which is correct there. But in my view the correct inference from the premises is: $v(p)$ and $v(q)$ do not exist. The further inference that therefore $v(p) = v(q)$ is of course not valid. So with respect to my biconditional it is to be noticed that

(a) $\underline{A} \equiv \underline{B} \;\Vdash\; \phi(A) \equiv \phi(B)$

(b) if $\underline{A}$ and $\underline{B}$ have the same value, so do $\phi(A)$ and $\phi(B)$, if either has a value,

both hold.[9] If the antecedent of (b) expresses what is meant by "materially equivalent," then there is no reason to hold that two truth-valueless sentences are thereby materially equivalent.

It may be worthwhile to explore another line of thought on this, in view of the claimed simplicity and convenience of matrices with their determinate—if sometimes unusual—calculations. Calculations of validity are the same for supervaluations as for the ordinary two-valued truth-tables: there I can claim the greater convenience. Calculations of contingent value—or lack thereof—of a complex statement on the basis of such information for its components is really not much more awkward. For example, let $\underline{p}$ and $\underline{q}$ alone among the atomic sentences have a truth-value, $\underline{p}$ true and $\underline{q}$ false. Then what is the value of $\underline{p} \supset (\underline{q} \vee \underline{r})$. ?

Simple:

$$
\begin{array}{cc|ccc}
\underline{p} & \supset & (q & \vee & r) \\
T & T & F & T & T \\
T & F & F & F & F \\
\end{array}
$$

since the main column shows both T's and F's, it has no value. We arrived at this result by assigning $<T, T>$ to $\underline{p}$, $<F, F>$ to $\underline{q}$, and $<T, F>$ to $\underline{r}$. More generally, order the classical valuations compatible with the objective situation in some way as $\underline{c}_1, \ldots, \underline{c}_\mu, \ldots$; assign to $\underline{A}$ the sequence $<\underline{c}_1(\underline{A}), \ldots, \underline{c}_\mu(\underline{A}), \ldots >$. Then the sequence assigned to ϕ $(\underline{p}_1, \ldots, \underline{p}_n)$ is $<\phi (\underline{d}_1^1, \ldots, \underline{d}_n^1), \ldots, \phi(\underline{d}_1^\mu, \ldots, \underline{d}_n^\mu), \ldots >$, where ϕ is the ordinary truth-function usually denoted as ϕ, and $<\underline{d}_i^1, \ldots, \underline{d}_i^\mu, \ldots >$ is the sequence assigned to $\underline{p}_i$, $\underline{i} = 1, \ldots, \underline{n}$. Thus treatment in terms of supervaluations is equivalent to treatment in terms of an infinite matrix, reducing in each specific case to treatment in terms of a finite matrix (of at

9. I am here indebted to clarifying discussions with P. Woodruff, University of California at Irvine, who had suggested that in some sense extensionality failed here.

most 2^{2^n} elements for a sentence with $\underline{n}$ atomic components).[10] I
have described the procedure abstractly, but the reader can ap-
ply it to any specific example once he has read the definition of
supervaluation: no new matrix operations need to be mastered.
This shows at once that there can be no philosophically significant difference between the use of matrices and the use of supervaluations, <u>and</u> that the latter are <u>at</u> <u>least</u> as simple and convenient as any matrix treatment.

10. This also follows immediately from the consideration that the set
of classical valuations can be regarded as an S_5-model structure, with the
supervaluation assigning T exactly to the sentences <u>necessary</u> in that structure (as was pointed out by Woodruff on another occasion) and Castañeda's
decision procedure in his "A Note on S_5," <u>Journal</u> <u>of</u> <u>Symbolic</u> <u>Logic</u>, 29
(1964), 191–92.

Notes on Quantification and Self-Reference

by Brian Skyrms

I have presented my solution to the Liar paradox in detail in a previous paper ("Return of the Liar: Three-Valued Logic and the Concept of Truth," American Philosophical Quarterly 7 [1970]: 153-61). The solution consisted in the development of a language in which some semantically self-referential sentences (including the Liar sentence) were expressible, in which some of these sentences were neither true nor false, and in which the fact that they were neither true nor false was expressible and in certain cases provable. This language, however, was an extremely primitive one which did not even contain quantifiers. The question arises as to whether similar results can be gotten for more interesting languages. The first step in this direction is the admission of first-order quantifiers. This step, however, leads to problems that I have not yet solved. What follows is therefore as much a description of what I am looking for, and where I am looking, as a report of what I have found.

Let me begin by outlining the results of the previous paper. We can set up the Liar paradox (what van Fraassen calls the Strengthened Liar paradox) very simply. Let the following sentence be true:

$$\underline{a} = \text{'}{\sim}T\underline{a}\text{'}$$

where the Liar sentence is the sentence '$\underline{a}$ is not true' ('${\sim}T\underline{a}$') and '$\underline{a}$' is the name of that sentence. Here we have the Liar naked. You sometimes encounter it with a lot more dressing, but the dressing always has to do with making the identity statement ('$\underline{a}$ = '${\sim}T\underline{a}$' ') true. To maintain that no such identity statement is ever true is to take up a rather desperate position, desperate because it is implausible on its face (with respect to a host of well-known examples) and uninteresting as a solution. (It is not surprising that refusal to recognize semantical self-reference will avoid the semantical paradoxes.) It seems to me, then, that such a position is a last ditch defense against contradiction, to be resorted to only if a theory of semantical self-reference should for some reason prove impossible. Therefore we work on the assumption that the identity statement is true.

Since I don't intend to wiggle out of difficulties by hedging on the truth of the identity sentence, I will further assume that all identity statements satisfy the law of bivalence. That is, all identity statements are either true or false. The Liar sentence itself is, however, a horse of a different color. Almost everyone wants to say that the Liar sentence ('~Ta') is neither true nor false, and that the perplexities it causes us result from our trying to handle such an exotic beast with procedures suitable only for more familiar bivalent animals.

The embarrassing fact is, however, that what nearly everyone wants to say appears to lead straight to a contradiction. Suppose that the Liar sentence is neither true nor false. Well, what it says is that it is not true, and therefore what it says is correct. But when a sentence says something that is correct, it is true. So the Liar sentence must be true, which contradicts our assumption.

I maintain that the foregoing argument contains a fallacy. The fallacy occurs when we say: "Well, if it isn't true, then what it says is correct." If the Liar sentence is meaningless, then it is indeed untrue. But it doesn't follow that what it says is correct, because if it is meaningless it doesn't say anything.

How does this work formally? If we start with:

(1) $\sim T$ '$\sim Ta$'

as an assumption we can substitute a different name of the same thing to get:

(2) $\sim Ta$.

But if the foregoing is true, then it is true to say it is true, so the move to:

(3) T '$\sim Ta$'

is valid. But this contradicts our assumption.

My position is that (1) is true; that (1) makes the correct claim that the Liar sentence is untrue. (2) however is untrue, for (2) is the Liar sentence itself. We got from (1) to (2) by means of the principle of substitutivity of identity, which must therefore be incorrect. But although it is incorrect, it is almost correct. It isn't as if (1) said something that was true, and (2) said a different thing that was false. Rather (1) says something that is true and (2) fails to say anything and is thus neither true nor false. The law of substitutivity of identity is valid in the weak sense that it can't take you from a true sentence to a false one, but it is not valid in the strong sense of always giving true conclusions from true premises. (I am, of course, not talking about substitution within quotation marks, which is invalid in all senses.) It follows that if we restrict ourselves to sentences that satisfy bivalence, substitutivity of identity is valid in the strong sense. The principle of substitutivity of identity, like the rest of classical logic, was developed to handle bivalent sentences, and it handles them without fault. It is not adequate to the strain of paradoxical sentences like the Liar.

The mere recognition that when there are meaningless sentences around, the move from (1) to (2) is not strongly valid, is enough to save us from contradiction. But it would be nice to have an explanation of why substitution of identities sometimes leads from a true sentence to a neuter one. I offer the following: We have the reason that what goes wrong with the Liar sentence and sentences like it is that there is a peculiar type of semantical self-reference going on that makes them meaningless. Notice that (1) isn't self-referential. It has the name of a sentence other than itself in it, the quotation-mark name of (2). But (2) is self-referential; it contains its own name. Substitutivity of identity took us from a true to a meaningless sentence by taking us from a non-self-referential one to a self-referential one. (2) is caught in a semantical trap which renders it incapable of making a meaningful assertion. The very fact that (2) is caught in this trap forms the basis for the truth of (1).

A word needs to be said about the differences between the failure of substitutivity of identity in self-referential contexts which I have been discussing, and the well-known failure of substitutivity of identity within the scope of modal, epistemic, and quotation functors. Quine argues that, when you don't have substitutivity of identity, then you are not really talking about the things you think you're talking about. But this conclusion is reached against a background assumption of bivalence. If substitutivity of identity fails within a bivalent context it really fails; it takes you from a truth to a falsehood. The failure I have been talking about is of a different order, and is a sign of something quite different. We are talking about sentences whenever we talk about anything. The point is that sometimes our attempt to talk about sentences aborts and we fail to talk about anything. But whenever we succeed in talking about something—that is, making a legitimate factual claim about something—we are talking about just what it seems we are talking about.

In my forthcoming article, "Return of the Liar," the ideas just outlined are incorporated in a rudimentary formal language. The language contains a truth-predicate, identity, quotation-mark names, and individual constants. One group of axioms guarantees that substitutivity of identity cannot lead from a truth to a falsehood. Another group guarantees that quotation-mark names are safe, that is, sentences containing only quotation-mark names satisfy bivalence The rationale for the latter group of axioms is that such sentences cannot be self-referential. The fact that (1) is true and (2) is neuter is expressible and provable in the language. There is a consistency proof.

When faced with self-referential paradoxes, there are two sorts of things you can do. You can simply construct a language in which self-reference doesn't happen. Let your logic be classical and your truth-predicate be global and nothing bad will happen. So you can have the no-self-reference solution, as I could have if I used only quotation-mark names in my language. Or you can have self-reference and introduce a third truth-value (or lack of truth-value) into the language and let the third value handle the paradoxes (as van Fraassen does). One way of looking at my solution is that I take these two approaches and put them together in one language. The way I put them together so that they are consistent is with the weakened rule of substitutivity of identity. And putting them together gives a whole that is in some sense greater than the sum of the parts, because now things can be done that can't be done on either of the other two approaches; that is, the contention that the Liar sentence is neither true nor false can be meaningfully expressed in the language and, furthermore, proven. The problem now is to do something like this with quantification theory. It is not solved but I can say a few things about it.

As a first timid step, suppose that we only take into our domain sentences of the elementary system just discussed. The domain will not, however, contain any quantificational sentences. We will have to make some sorts of modifications of quantification theory even to take this step. Suppose again that $\underline{a} = '\sim T\underline{a}'$, so that '$\sim T\underline{a}$' is a Liar sentence. Consider the following two quantified sentences:

$$(\alpha): \quad (\underline{x}) \, (\underline{x} = '\sim T\underline{a}' \supset \sim T\underline{x})$$
$$(\beta): \quad (\underline{x}) \, (\underline{x} = \underline{a} \supset \sim T\underline{x}).$$

Each of them, on the face of it, appears to say that the Liar sentence is untrue. There is always the possibility that, contrary to appearances, these sentences, like the Liar sentence itself, are meaningless. But it is clear that, if meaningful, they must be true. It is to be hoped that we can retain at least one of them as meaningful. But if so, we cannot retain universal specification as strongly valid. For from (α) we can specify to:

$$\underline{a} = '\sim T\underline{a}' \supset \sim T\underline{a}$$

and then detach to get the Liar sentence, while from (β) we can specify to:

$$\underline{a} = \underline{a} \supset \sim T\underline{a}$$

and again detach to get the Liar sentence. Thus, assuming that either (α) or (β) is meaningful, universal specification has taken us from a true to a meaningless sentence. (I am assuming that the semantics of molecular sentences is handled by supervaluations, so that each of the foregoing conditionals would be neuter.) So far, however, we can say that it is valid in the weak sense of not leading from a truth to a falsehood, just as we did with substitution of identity. This again gives the desired result that the rules of classical logic continue to hold for bivalent sentences. Another way of putting it is to say that to be strongly valid, universal specification requires an additional premise to the effect that the sentence specified to is either true or false.

We would of course maintain the universal validity of universal specification against this counterexample by holding that both (α) and (β) are meaningless, but this course is highly implausible. Since quantificational sentences are excluded from the domain, (α) and (β) cannot be self-referential. If we believe that meaninglessness is caused by a particular type of semantical self-reference, then we must hold that (α) and (β) are true. This forces us to admit that universal specification is not strongly valid, but it also provides us with an explanation of just what goes wrong when universal specification leads us from a true to a meaningless sentence. In both cases cited, universal specification led from a non-self-referential sentence to a molecule containing a self-referential atomic sentence (i.e. the Liar sentence). The situation here is quite analogous to the situation with respect to substitutivity of identity.

So much for the first timid step. Suppose that we now admit quantificational sentences themselves into the domain. We can now have a quantificational sentence that claims itself to be untrue. For instance if $\underline{b}$ = '$(\underline{x})(\underline{x} = \underline{b} \supset {\sim}T\underline{x})$', it is then easy to show that the quantificational Liar sentence:

(γ): $(\underline{x})(\underline{x} = \underline{b} \supset {\sim}T\underline{x})$

is neither true nor false. Suppose it is true. From (γ) we get:

'$(\underline{x})(\underline{x} = \underline{b} \supset {\sim}T\underline{x})$ = $\underline{b} \supset {\sim}T$ $(\underline{x})(\underline{x} = \underline{b} \supset {\sim}T\underline{x})$'.

But this sentence must be either true or false, since its antecedent is an identity statement and its consequent is the denial of a truth ascription statement containing a quotation-mark name. So universal specification is licensed here, and the result must be true. Its antecedent is true, thus so must be its consequent. But the consequent contradicts the assumption that (γ) is true. Suppose, on the other hand, that (γ) is false. Then its denial:

($\exists\underline{x}$)($\underline{x} = \underline{b}$ & $T\underline{x}$)

must be true. For it to be true there must be something in the domain that satisfies both conjuncts; that is, something _is_ the quantificational Liar sentence and is true. We have just shown this to be impossible.

The question arises as to whether (γ)'s lack of truth-value can be attributed to its containing the name, 'b', and whether it might not be the case that pure quantificational sentences without any singular referring terms satisfy bivalence. The answer is no because you can get into the same sort of trouble using descriptions. Suppose that you have some syntactical predicate, 'ϕ', such that '$\phi\underline{x}$' is satisfied only by the sentence, '$(\underline{x})(\phi\underline{x} \supset {\sim}T\underline{x})$'. Here '$\phi\underline{x}$' takes the place of '$\underline{x} = \underline{b}$' in the former example. Much the same reasoning shows that this Liar sentence can be neither true nor false. (The formal proof is a bit longer, and thus there are more steps that might be rejected, but it isn't plausible to reject any of them.)

Remember that in the elementary language we put "safe" quotation-mark name sentences that were incapable of self-reference together with dangerous individual constant sentences by means of weakened substitutivity of identity. And in our timid halfway quantificational language we put "safe" quantificational sentences together with unsafe sentences with weakened universal specification. Now that pure quantificational sentences are capable of pathological self-reference, the question arises as to what is safe. "Safe" up to now has been something that precludes self-reference. But as it now stands, we are quantifying over all sentences. So it looks as though every sentence is self-referential and nothing is safe.

I think the answer is that although a quantificational sentence is about everything, it is not about everything in the relevant way all the time. What is dangerous is not self-reference per se but a particular type of semantical self-reference. A quantificational sentence might contain some syntactical predicates which, together with the structure of the sentence, tell us that there are lots of sentences in the domain whose semantical properties are irrelevant to the truth of the sentence in question. The semantical properties of other sentences in the domain are relevant. For instance, in our example:

$$(\epsilon): \quad (\underline{x})(\phi\underline{x} \supset {\sim}T\underline{x}),$$

given the information that just one sentence has the syntactical property ϕ, we are then in the position that only the truth-value of that sentence is relevant in deciding the truth-value of (ϵ). I shall say that (ϵ) is semantically about those sentences that satisfy '$\phi\underline{x}$'. In the version of the pure quantificational Liar that we considered, (ϵ) was semantically about just itself.

If you accept this as the relevant sort of self-reference, then we can have some "safe" non-self-referential sentences. (Actually, the definition of semantical-aboutness and semantical self-reference in terms of it would be a bit complicated. The preceding is to be taken as an indication of the basic idea rather than as a definition.)

The question now arises as to whether the ghost of the (Strengthened) Liar haunts us in quantification theory. We have proved that (γ) and (ϵ) are neither true nor false, but might not this conclusion also lead to a contradiction? I will discuss the question with respect to (γ). The situation with respect to (ϵ) is not different in any essential respects. I should mention at this point that I am assuming that all the universally valid formulas of classical quantification theory with identity remain universally valid. One might suppose that this would conflict with weakened substitutivity of identity, but this is not the case. The restriction on universal specification allows us to retain the theory of identity in its classical form in pure quantification theory. The following is a theorem:

$$(\underline{x})\,(\underline{y})\,(\sim T\underline{x} \mathbin{\&} \underline{x} = \underline{y} \supset \sim T\underline{y})$$

but we can't specify to:

$$\sim T\;\text{'}\sim T\underline{a}\text{'} \mathbin{\&} \underline{a} = \text{'}\sim T\underline{a}\text{'} \supset \sim T\underline{a}$$

because such specification requires an extra premise to the effect that the sentence specified to is either true or false. And that sentence is not either true or false. As a conditional having a true antecedent and a meaningless consequent, it is meaningless.

The idea behind trying to get the Liar back in quantification theory is to use the theory of identity in a more devious way to gain the same effect. Consider the following:

(1) $\sim T\;\text{'}(\underline{x})\,(\underline{x} = \underline{b} \supset \sim T\underline{x})\text{'}$ Assume

(2) $(\underline{x})\,(\sim T\underline{x} \supset (\underline{y})\,(\underline{y} = \underline{x} \supset \sim T\underline{y}))$ Theory of Identity

(3) $\sim T\;\text{'}(\underline{x})\,(\underline{x} = \underline{b} \supset \sim T\underline{x})\text{'} \supset (\underline{y})\,(\underline{y} = \text{'}(\underline{x})\,(\underline{x} = \underline{b} \supset \sim T\underline{x})\text{'} \supset \sim T\underline{y})$ 2/U.S.

(4) $(\underline{y})\,(\underline{y} = \text{'}(\underline{x})\,(\underline{x} = \underline{b} \supset \sim T\underline{x})\text{'} \supset \sim T\underline{y})$ 1,3/Detach.

(5) $(\underline{x})\,(\underline{y})\,(\underline{x} = \underline{y} \supset (\underline{z})\,(\underline{z} = \underline{x} \supset \underline{z} = \underline{y}))$ Theory of Identity

(6) $b = \text{'}(\underline{x})\,(\underline{x} = \underline{b} \supset \sim T\underline{x})\text{'} \supset (\underline{z})\,(\underline{z} = \underline{b} \supset \underline{z} = \text{'}(\underline{x})\,(\underline{x} = \underline{b} \supset \sim T\underline{x})\text{'})$ 5/U.S.

(7) $\underline{b} = \text{'}(\underline{x})\,(\underline{x} = \underline{b} \supset \sim T\underline{x})\text{'}$ Given

(8) $(\underline{z})\,(\underline{z} = \underline{b} \supset \underline{z} = \text{'}(\underline{x})\,(\underline{x} = \underline{b} \supset \sim T\underline{x})\text{'})$ 6,7/Detach.

(9) $(\underline{y})\,(\underline{y} = \underline{b} \supset \sim T\underline{y})$ 4,8 Quant. Theory

(10) $(\underline{x})\,(\underline{x} = \underline{b} \supset \sim T\underline{x})$ Relettering

From the assumption that the quantificational Liar sentence is untrue, I have derived the quantificational Liar sentence itself. The universal specification steps should be all right because, given previous conjectures, the sentences specified to must be either true or false. There must be a fallacy somewhere in the proof, and I claim that it occurs right at the end — in the step from (9) to (10). I maintain that (9) is a perfectly legitimate way of claiming that the quantificational Liar sentence is untrue, and thus (9) is true. (10), being the quantificational Liar sentence itself, is neither true nor false. Relettering took us from a true to a neuter sentence and thus is not strongly valid but rather in the same boat as substitutivity of identity and universal specification. The reason relettering took us from a true sentence to a neuter one should be familiar; it also took us from a non-self-referential sentence to a self-referential one (in the sense of self-reference sketched on p. 72.

But couldn't we have smuggled in the variable '$\underline{x}$' earlier in the proof and thus gotten the undesirable result without explicit use of a rule of relettering? Consider the following variation on the preceding derivation:

(2') $(\underline{y}) (\sim T\underline{y} \supset (\underline{x}) (\underline{x} = \underline{y} \supset \sim T\underline{x}))$ Theory of Identity
(3') $\sim T$ '$(\underline{x}) (\underline{x} = \underline{b} \supset \sim T\underline{x})$' $\supset (\underline{x}) (x = $'$(\underline{x}) (\underline{x} = \underline{b} \supset \sim Tx)$'$\supset \sim T\underline{x})$
                                                                2'/U.S.

From (3'), it is easy enough to get to (10) by legitimate steps. The only conclusion possible is that (3') is neither true nor false, and thus that the step from (2') to (3') is not a legitimate universal specification. Since the antecedent of (3') is true, the consequent must be meaningless.

Although the consequent of (3') is not explicitly self-referential, it is apparently too close for safety. We would like some sort of general characterization of what went wrong. I suggest that we can take the problem to be that the bound variable '$\underline{x}$' occurs <u>both</u> <u>outside</u> <u>and</u> <u>within</u> <u>the</u> <u>quotation</u> <u>marks</u> and occurs in conjunction with a <u>semantical</u> <u>predicate</u>, 'T', outside the quotation marks. When universal specification to a quotation-mark name makes both these things happen, it is illicit. On the other hand, I would hold that the sentence:

(8') $(\underline{x}) (\underline{x} = \underline{b} \supset \underline{x} = $'$(\underline{x}) (\underline{x} = \underline{b} \supset \sim T\underline{x})$'$)$

is true, for it is an identity sentence, rather than a semantical one.

It seems clear that it would be very hard to stay out of trouble if one granted that both (3') and (8') were true, so things must be stopped earlier. The only viable alternative to the preceding tack, as far as I can see, is a modification of the theory of identity that would be consistent with saying that (2) and (2') are neither true nor false.

The decision as to which alternative is best will await some systematic work in syntax and semantics.

Comments and a Suggestion

by Frederic B. Fitch

Skyrms has constructed a consistent system that avoids the Epimenides paradox but lacks quantifiers, and he has sketched another system that also avoids the Epimenides paradox but contains quantifiers. One aspect of these systems that I would object to is the sacrifice of substitutivity with respect to identity. This seems to me too high a price to pay even to get rid of the Epimenides paradox. I cannot accept the idea that there are three truth-values for sentences—true, false, and neuter—and that something $\underline{a}$ can be identical with something $\underline{b}$, and yet some sentence can be true of $\underline{a}$ but only neuter of $\underline{b}$, even where $\underline{a}$ and $\underline{b}$ are referred to by proper names rather than by descriptive phrases. This situation, that a sentence is true of $\underline{a}$ but only neuter of $\underline{b}$, seems to me to indicate a difference between $\underline{a}$ and $\underline{b}$ and to belie the claim that $\underline{a}$ is completely identical with $\underline{b}$.

I believe that there is a simple solution to the Epimenides paradox, and one that does not require any fundamental modification of classical two-valued logic or any rejection of substitutivity with respect to identity, and which does not invoke the branched theory of types.

The essential idea is that the application of a predicate to a well-formed sentence (or to a name of a proposition) does not always give a well-formed sentence as a result. Suppose a predicate, say '$\underline{P}$', is thought of as referring to a property of propositions, and a well-formed sentence (or name of a proposition), say '$\underline{s}$', is thought of as referring to a proposition, while the result '$\underline{P}(\underline{s})$' of applying '$\underline{P}$' to '$\underline{s}$' is thought of as a sentence to the effect that the proposition referred to by '$\underline{s}$' has the property referred to by '$\underline{P}$'. The claim I wish to make is that for some choices of predicate and sentence, the result '$\underline{P}(\underline{s})$' may not be a well-formed sentence and so may not express a proposition. In particular, this failure to produce a well-formed sentence might arise if the predicate is an empirically defined predicate, for example such as the predicate: "is referred to by notation on the blackboard at 1834 Silliman College." One way of apparently obtaining the Epimenides paradox is to use the latter predicate to form the following "sentence": "Every proposition referred to by the notation on the blackboard at 1834 Silliman College is false," where this "sentence" itself is the only notation on the blackboard in question. This "sentence," if formalized in the notation of symbolic logic, could be written

$$(\underline{x})_{\underline{R}}{\sim}\underline{x}$$

where '$\underline{R}$' is the predicate that expresses the property of being a proposition referred to by notation on the blackboard at 1834 Silliman College, and where '$(\underline{x})_{\underline{R}}$' is a restricted universal quantifier that can be read as "for all $\underline{x}$ having property $\underline{R}$." Thus if '$(\underline{x})_{\underline{R}}{\sim}\underline{x}$' were a well-formed sentence, it would mean that everything that has property $\underline{R}$ is false, so that the proposition expressed by such a sentence would be asserting itself to be false. The claim I make is that the expression '$(\underline{x})_{\underline{R}}{\sim}\underline{x}$' can be considered not to be a well-formed sentence. In general, if '$\underline{P}$' is a predicate, then an expression of the form '$(\underline{x})_{\underline{P}}(. . . \underline{x} . . .)$' is well-formed, on my view, only if each expression of the form '$(. . . \underline{s} . . .)$' is well-formed for each well-formed sentence '$\underline{s}$' that is such that '$\underline{P}(\underline{s})$' is both well-formed and true (expresses a true proposition); while if there is no such '$\underline{s}$' that can be used to form a well-formed instantiation of '$(\underline{x})_{\underline{P}}(. . . \underline{x} . . .)$', the latter may be said not to be well-formed. Now the property expressed by '$\underline{R}$' applies to at most one proposition, because on the blackboard in question there is reference to at most one proposition and possibly to none. Furthermore, whether or not '$(\underline{x})_{\underline{R}}{\sim}\underline{x}$' is a well-formed sentence, it is possible to take the position that '$\underline{R}((\underline{x})_{\underline{R}}{\sim}\underline{x})$' is not a well-formed sentence since '$\underline{R}$' is an empirically defined predicate rather than a purely logically defined one. But if '$\underline{R}((\underline{x})_{\underline{R}}{\sim}\underline{x})$' is not a well-formed sentence, then neither is '$(\underline{x})_{\underline{R}}{\sim}\underline{x}$', because the latter would have no well-formed instantiation '${\sim}\underline{s}$'. In other words, there would be no proposition having the property expressed by '$\underline{R}$' and hence no proposition that could be used to construct an instantiation by way of a sentence expressing such a proposition. If '$(\underline{x})_{\underline{R}}{\sim}\underline{x}$' fails to be a well-formed sentence and if it (or its ordinary-language equivalent) is what is written on the blackboard, then no proposition is being referred to by the notation on the blackboard, and the Epimenides paradox is avoided. Even if in place of '$(\underline{x})_{\underline{R}}{\sim}\underline{x}$' we use '$(\underline{x})[{\sim}\underline{R}(\underline{x}) \text{ v } {\sim}\underline{x}]$', where the universal quantifier now refers to all propositions, we still need not view '$(\underline{x})[{\sim}\underline{R}(\underline{x}) \text{ v } {\sim}\underline{x}]$' as a well-formed sentence, because to do so according to our principles would presuppose that '${\sim}\underline{R}(\underline{s}) \text{ v } {\sim}\underline{s}$' is a well-formed sentence for every well-formed sentence '$\underline{s}$', and this in turn would presuppose that '$\underline{R}(\underline{s})$' is a well-formed sentence for every well-formed sentence '$\underline{s}$', which is the very point that I am inclined to deny.

Just as it is an empirical matter as to which propositions have which empirically defined properties, so also it is, on my view, an empirical matter as to which empirically defined predicates can be attached to which well-formed sentences so as to give well-formed sentences—though I would assume that all logically defined predicates give well-formed sentences when so attached. In cases where contradictions arise from allowing attachments of empirically defined predicates to give well-formed sentences, as in the case of the Epimenides paradox, the well-formed character of the resulting expression can be denied, and so there is no resulting well-formed sentence to cause trouble. This way of avoiding the paradox is consistent both with classical two-valued logic and with the principle of substitutivity with respect to identity.

The Truth about Truth: A Reply to Brian Skyrms

by John L. Pollock

I

Skyrms has made a number of fascinating suggestions regarding the Liar paradox. He quite rightly objects that the Tarski language levels approach to the Liar paradox is intuitively unsatisfying. It does not seem reasonable to say that we have different truth-concepts at each language level. Intuitively we want to say that each of these stratified truth-concepts is simply a restriction of a single global concept of truth. Consequently Skyrms is led to inquire what sorts of formal moves would allow us to salvage a global concept of truth. In "Return of the Liar," in which he only considers unquantified semantical sentences, he concludes that by saying that the Liar sentence is neither true nor false, and by denying the substitutivity of identity in truth-contexts, we can have a "mildly global" truth concept, in the sense that given any sentence, there is some description of it to which we can append 'is true' and obtain a meaningful sentence. He calls this the "modified Chrysippian solution." In "Notes on Quantification and Self-Reference" Skyrms considers how the remarks of his earlier paper may be extended to deal with quantified semantical sentences, making a number of interesting observations. However, the peg upon which he hangs the rest of his theory is that substitutivity of identity fails in truth-contexts. I feel that this basic unelaborated position must be discussed more thoroughly before we proceed to extend it to the problems that arise in connection with quantification.

A formal analysis of the sort given by Skyrms can be quite suggestive, but it does not by itself constitute a solution to the Liar paradox. A solution to the Liar paradox must consist of an explanation of the meaning of 'true' and a demonstration that, given that analysis of 'true', the Liar sentence is not paradoxical. Formal investigations concerned with what sorts of restrictions we might make to our ordinary reasoning that would prevent the derivation of a contradiction from the Liar sentence may point the way to an analysis of 'true' that would solve the paradox. But such a formal investigation by itself does not constitute a solution—it is not a foregone conclusion that, given an arbitrary formal solution, there will be a reasonable analysis of 'true' that is in accordance with that formal solution.

Let us ask whether a reasonable analysis of truth can be found that leads to the formal restrictions proposed by Skyrms. In order to lead to those restrictions, such an analysis must make $\ulcorner p$ is true$\urcorner$ referentially opaque, because unrestricted substitutivity is supposed to fail in truth-contexts.[1] This observation by itself suffices to show that Skyrms' proposals are incompatible with most traditional theories of truth. For example the correspondence theory of truth asserts, roughly, that a sentence is true iff it "corresponds to the facts." But in $\ulcorner p$ corresponds to the facts$\urcorner$, p is functioning purely referentially. Consequently, on this analysis truth-contexts are referentially transparent. Analogously, the coherence and pragmatic theories of truth (although I am sure Skyrms would wish to endorse neither) are incompatible with Skyrms' proposals.

Many philosophers have wanted to say that the concept of truth applies first to propositions, and insofar as it makes sense to ascribe truth to sentences, this must be a derivative sense of 'true' which means 'expresses a true proposition'. On this analysis, letting 'p' range over sentences and 'ϕ' range over propositions, 'Tp' means '$(\exists\phi)[E(p, \phi)$ & $T\phi]$'. Then the only way that 'Tp' can be referentially opaque is if '$E(p, \phi)$' is referentially opaque with respect to 'p'. The referential opacity of truth for propositions would not make truth referentially opaque for sentences. But now, is it plausible to suppose that '$E(p, \phi)$' is referentially opaque? I do not think so. To say that a sentence p expresses a proposition ϕ seems merely to be saying something about the existence of certain rules of language that determine the meaning of p. Such a statement is not referentially opaque. It <u>might</u> be possible to explain the meaning of 'p expresses the proposition ϕ' in such a way that it becomes referentially opaque, but I cannot now see any way of doing so.

This does not constitute a very serious objection to Skyrms' proposals, because one could with a certain amount of plausibility object that talking about propositions here is simply wrongheaded —talk about sentences is basic and talk about propositions is to be analyzed in terms of talk about sentences. Many philosophers have

---

1. Because of the failure of bivalence, this is not quite the classical concept of referential opacity. Nevertheless, it should be noted that this makes the sort of quantification into truth-contexts that Skyrms discusses very suspicious. It is hard to understand what such quantifiers might mean, so it is not particularly surprising that they lead to some strange results.

held such a position. But then we are still faced with the problem
of explaining what it means to say that a sentence is true and showing that such an analysis makes ⌜p is true⌝ referentially opaque.
I can see no way to do that.

Still, I think one must agree that the Liar sentence is meaningless, and hence that <u>some</u> form of the Chrysippian solution must
work. But as Skyrms remarks, the simple observation that the
Liar sentence is meaningless is not sufficient to block the paradox,
because one can always turn to the Strengthened liar sentence,
which says of itself that it is either false or meaningless. If one
says that this sentence is meaningless, he is again faced with the
full force of the paradox. However, I think there is a way of avoiding this. I want to make some suggestions that lead to a solution
to the Liar paradox that is different from Skyrms' solution but
related to it in that it too embodies a modified Chrysippian approach.

II

The Liar paradox turns around the word 'true', so let us examine
that word. 'true' is used in English both as a predicate and as an
operator. That is, we may say either (1) 'What he said is true' or
'The sentence at the bottom of the page is true', or (2) 'It is true
that it is going to rain'. Philosophers have generally restricted
their attention to the predicate use in giving theories of truth.
Presumably, one of these two uses is basic, and the other logically derived from it. And there seems to be a good reason for thinking that the operator use of 'true' is the basic one. This is that no
paradoxes can be generated if we only use 'true' as an operator,
because 'it is true that' is always eliminable from a sentence in
which it occurs. It is essential to the Liar paradox that 'true' be
used as a predicate in the Liar sentence.

The operator use of 'true' need not be taken as primitive; it
is easily defined. When appended to the front of an English indicative sentence, 'It is true that' yields a new English indicative sentence the meaning of which can be characterized by saying that it
is the same as that of the original sentence. So we define: ⌜It is
true that p⌝ = $_{df}$ p. So far, no paradox. Now it seems that we can
introduce the predicate use of 'true' in two steps. First we define
the predicate use as applied to the quotation names of sentences:
⌜'p' is true⌝ = $_{df}$ ⌜It is true that p⌝ (= $_{df}$ p). We then define more
generally, where $\underline{a}$ is any term denoting a sentence:

$$⌜\underline{a} \text{ is true}⌝ = _{df} ⌜(\exists \underline{p})(\underline{a} = \text{'}\underline{p}\text{'} \ \& \ \text{'}\underline{p}\text{' is true})⌝.$$

This latter definition appears to involve a confusion between use and mention. In order for it to work, the variable p̲ must be construed as a schematic letter rather than a variable in the ordinary sense, and the quantifier construed as a sort of generalized disjunction operator. A lengthy discussion of such an interpretation of quantifiers can be found in the literature. No attempt will be made here to ascertain whether such quantifiers are legitimate. Let us simply suppose for now that they are. If they are not, it is hard to see how 'true' could be introduced as a predicate.[2]

Notice that the above definition of the predicate use of 'true' leads to the result that ⌜p is true⌝ is meaningful iff p̲ itself is. Thus if we agree that the Liar sentence L is meaningless, we are led to the conclusion that both 'TL' and '~TL' are meaningless. This is very close to van Fraassen's solution to the Liar paradox ("Presuppositions, Implication, and Self-Reference," The Journal of Philosophy, 65 (1968), 136–51). Skyrms' main objection (in "Return of the Liar") to this solution seems to be the "ineffability problem" that

$$T \text{ '~TL' v } T \text{ '~~TL' v } (\sim T \text{ '~TL' \& } \sim T \text{ '~~TL'})$$

is true but no disjunct is true. However, Skyrms has his own ineffability problem. On his solution, 'TL v ~TL' is true but neither disjunct is true. I submit that neither ineffability problem is real. They both result from taking the supervaluation approach to three-valued logic. As van Fraassen remarks, when using supervaluations tautologies cannot be read in the way we are accustomed to reading them.

The observation that ⌜Tp⌝ is meaningful iff p̲ is meaningful solves the Liar paradox very nicely. Unfortunately, it does not solve the Strengthened Liar paradox. It is essential to the above solution that there be a predicate 'meaningless', because an essential part of that solution is to say that the Liar sentence is meaningless. 'Meaningless' cannot be taken to mean 'neither true nor false', because that conjunction is itself meaningless when applied to a meaningless sentence like the Liar sentence. Thus there must be a primitive predicate 'meaningless'. But then it is a simple matter

2. Skyrms has pointed out to me that there are problems with these quantifiers. Using them it is possible to construct a Liar sentence without using a truth-predicate; we need merely construct a sentence a̲ such that a̲ = '(p̲)[‘p̲’ = a̲ ⊃ ~p̲]'. One way out of this difficulty would be to require that these quantifiers only range over regular sentences (see section IV). But this is merely a suggestion. Clearly, more needs to be said about these quantifiers.

to construct a new sentence that says of itself that it is either false or meaningless. This gives us the Strengthened Liar paradox all over again.

III

It seems to me that the Liar paradox arises from not taking seriously the difference between a predicate and an operator. This difference is important. To illustrate this in more neutral territory, Richard Montague ("Syntactical Treatments of Modality, with Corollaries on Reflexion Principles and Finite Axiomatizability," Acta Philosophica Fennica, 16 (1963), 153–68) has proven a theorem that tells us essentially that there can be no predicate 'is logically necessary' related to the modal operator 'it is logically necessary that' in such a way that

> $\ulcorner$'$\underline{p}$' is logically necessary $\equiv$ it is logically necessary that $\underline{p}$ $\urcorner$

always holds. Montague proved that if a reasonably expressive theory contained such a predicate and it satisfied the minimal set of axioms of S1, one of the weakest of all modal logics, that theory would be inconsistent. But it cannot reasonably be denied that S1 is sound — it is so weak that anyone should accept it. Consequently, the modal operator of logical necessity cannot be replaced by a predicate. Bringing things closer back to the Liar paradox, one can prove analogously that there can be no predicate corresponding to the operator of logical negation, and similarly that there can be no two-place predicate corresponding to conjunction. In either case we could derive a contradiction akin to the Liar paradox.

In defining a predicate on the basis of an operator, we employ definitions of the general form: $\ulcorner$F'$\underline{p}$'$\urcorner$ = $_{df}$ $\ulcorner$$f\underline{p}$$\urcorner$, where '$f$' is the operator and 'F' is the predicate. Such a definition goes from the use of a sentence to the mention of that sentence. Let us call a definition that has this characteristic a "type-crossing" definition. It is not immediately obvious that type-crossing definitions are legitimate. A mode of definition is something that must be justified. This is done by showing that the mode of definition always succeeds in isolating a unique concept or object. For example, in set theory we justify definitions by transfinite recursion by proving that there is always a unique class satisfying the clauses of the recursion.

A definition of a concept must provide us with a way of reducing, in a finite number of steps, the question whether an object exemplifies that concept, to other questions we already understand. If a definition does provide us with such a reduction, then clearly it has provided a meaning for the definiendum and hence is a legitimate definition. Conversely, if the definition provides no such reduction, then it gives us no way to determine whether an object exemplifies the concept and hence provides no meaning for the definiendum.

The simplest kind of definition is an explicit definition. An explicit definition has the form: $\ulcorner \underline{Fx} \urcorner = {}_{df} \ulcorner \ldots \underline{x} \ldots \urcorner$. Here we simply identify the meaning of $\ulcorner \underline{Fx} \urcorner$ with the meaning of some more complicated sentence about $\underline{x}$. It is obvious that a predicate introduced by an explicit definition can always be eliminated from any context in which it occurs simply by replacing it with its definition, so there is never any problem about the legitimacy of an explicit definition.

A type-crossing definition looks superficially like an explicit definition, but it isn't one. In an explicit definition we are predicating something of $\underline{x}$ in both the definiens and the definiendum, but this is not the case in a type-crossing definition. Consequently, if type-crossing definitions are to be legitimate, they must be justified. It is a simple matter to show that they cannot be justified. The reason the Liar sentence is paradoxical is precisely because the purported type-crossing definition of "true" provides no way to determine whether the Liar sentence is true. If it did, no paradox would ensue. Consequently, type-crossing definitions of the above general form are illegitimate.

If the definition of a term provides no way to determine whether a sentence containing that term is true, then the definition was illegitimate and the sentence meaningless.[3] Consequently the Liar sentence is meaningless. So far we agree with Chrysippus, Skyrms, van Fraassen, and the angels. But this observation by itself is not sufficient to solve the Liar paradox. It leaves the field open for the Strengthened Liar paradox. And in fact, it seems to lead to a generalized paradox involving any predicate purportedly introduced by a type-crossing definition. Suppose 'F' is such a predicate. Then using a standard diagonal construction we can construct a sentence $\underline{p}$ that says of itself that it is either F or meaningless: $\underline{p}$ = '$F\underline{p}$ v $\underline{p}$ is meaningless'. There is no way to determine whether $\underline{p}$ is F, so the first disjunct must be meaningless. If $\underline{p}$ were true, then it would have to be the second disjunct that is true, in which case $\underline{p}$ would be meaningless. Hence $\underline{p}$ could not be true. Nor could

---

3. To say that a sentence is meaningless is to say that rules for its use do not exist. If the definition of some term in the sentence is illegitimate, then a fortiori we have not succeeded in providing rules for the use of the sentence.

p̲ be false because then both disjuncts would have to be false,
whereas the first is meaningless. Thus p̲ must be meaningless.
But then p̲ satisfies the condition 'either is F or is meaningless',
and hence is true. But then p̲ is not meaningless—a contradiction.

The conclusion we must draw from this is that, because the
definition of 'F' is illegitimate, <u>any</u> sentence in which 'F' is used
is meaningless. Thus from 'p̲ is meaningless' we cannot conclude
'F̲p̲ or p̲ is meaningless', because the latter sentence is itself
meaningless. That this is so is really rather obvious. Presumably the sentence '$\sqrt{2}$ is red' is meaningless. Now consider the
sentence 'Either $\sqrt{2}$ is red or John is in the barn'. If we say that
a disjunction is true if one disjunct is true and the other meaningless, but meaningless if one disjunct is false and the other meaningless, then the question of whether the above sentence is meaningless
turns on the nonlinguistic question of whether John is in the barn.
But this is absurd. The meaningfulness of a sentence is a linguistic
matter, independent of the contingent truth or falsity of the constituents of the sentence. Consequently, if one constituent of a sentence
is meaningless, then the sentence itself must be meaningless. This
involves rejecting not only the supervaluation approach to the semantics of molecular sentences, but also the more modest proposal
(found for example in Martin's paper in this volume) that a disjunction is true when at least one disjunct is true, even if the other disjunct is meaningless.

IV

My conclusion so far is that if we pay attention to the difference
between operators and predicates, we can see that type-crossing
definitions of the simple sort discussed above are illegitimate, and
hence the Liar sentence is meaningless and the Strengthened Liar
paradox cannot be gotten off the ground either. If this were taken
as implying that we cannot construct a predicate use of 'true', it
would surely be wrong, because English contains such a predicate
use of 'true'. Fortunately, we can show that there are other kinds
of type-crossing definitions that are legitimate, and the predicate
use of 'true' can be introduced in that way.

The simplest kind of legitimate type-crossing definition is the
following:

$$\ulcorner F`p'\urcorner =_{df} \ulcorner f\underline{p}\urcorner \quad \text{(provided 'F' does not occur in } \underline{p} \text{).}$$

Here the range of meaningful applicability of 'F' is restricted to
those sentences in which 'F' does not occur. Such a type-crossing
definition is obviously legitimate, because the defined term 'F' can
always be eliminated from any sentence in which it is used: $\ulcorner \underline{Fa}\urcorner$

is equivalent to $\ulcorner(\exists p)[\underline{`p'} = \underline{a} \ \& \ f\underline{p}]\urcorner$. In this way we can define a predicate use of 'true' that can be ascribed meaningfully to any sentence in which that predicate is not used. We can then repeat the process, defining a more comprehensive predicate 'true$_2$' whose range of meaningful applicability contains all of the sentences in which it itself is not used, i.e. all of the sentences we started with together with all of the sentences in which 'true' is used. We can repeat this process indefinity getting a hierarchy of truth-predicates. This is just the Tarski language level approach. It results from using what is no doubt the simplest kind of legitimate type-crossing definition.

But it is frequently objected to the language level approach that intuitively all of these truth-predicates are restrictions of a single more general predicate. This objection is further supported by the observation that the predicate 'true' in English is not fragmented in this way. That such fragmentation is unnecessary results from the fact that a somewhat more complicated kind of type-crossing definition can be shown to be legitimate. This kind of definition is recursive and deals with sentences not containing quantifiers. (For the present I will make no attempt to deal with quantified semantical sentences.) Let us begin with all sentences in which 'true' is not used as a predicate. Then we define recursively:

1. $\underline{p}$ is a sentence of type 0 iff $\underline{p}$ is a meaningful sentence and 'true' is not used as a predicate in $\underline{p}$.
2. If $\underline{p}$ is an unquantified sentence (i.e. unquantified and syntactically well-formed but not necessarily meaningful) and the highest type of any sentence occurring in $\underline{p}$ (other than simply mentioned in $\underline{p}$) is $\underline{n}$, then $\underline{p}$ is of type $\underline{n}$.
3. If $\underline{p}$ is an unquantified sentence of type $\underline{n}$, then $\ulcorner `\underline{p}'$ is true$\urcorner$ is a sentence of type $\underline{n}+1$.

Let us say that a sentence is <u>regular</u> if it has a type. Then we can give a definition of a predicate use of 'true' for any regular sentence:

If $\underline{p}$ is a regular sentence, then $\ulcorner `\underline{p}'$ is true$\urcorner = {}_{df} \underline{p}$.

That this kind of type-crossing definition is legitimate is evidenced by the fact that given any sentence of some type $\underline{n}$, and given the truth-values of the parts of the sentence not involving 'true', we can determine the truth value of $\ulcorner `\underline{p}'$ is true$\urcorner$ in $\underline{n}+1$ steps.

This definition gives us an "almost global" truth-predicate — a single truth-predicate that is defined for all <u>meaningful</u> (unquantified) English sentences. But this truth-predicate is simply not defined for such meaningless sentences as the Liar sentence. However, we need not stop here. We can extend the definition so that 'true' is defined for all sentences — we need merely stipulate that if a sentence is not regular then it is false (i.e. untrue). This gives us a global truth-predicate. However, when 'true' is so defined, the Tarski schema $\ulcorner T'p' \equiv p \urcorner$ fails when p is not regular. For example, if 'p' is the Liar sentence then we have both p and $\sim T'p'$. From the assertion of the Liar sentence we cannot infer its truth because it is not regular. Thus the Liar sentence is simply false and no paradox threatens. I submit that the above definition gives us the meaning of the predicate use of 'true' in English for unquantified semantical sentences. This blocks all forms of the Liar paradox.

We can also show that this solution also blocks the more general paradox mentioned above. Just as for truth, we can define recursively a predicate '$\underline{F}$' by stipulating that $\ulcorner \underline{F}'p' \urcorner =_{df} \ulcorner \mathcal{f}p \urcorner$ or 'p' is meaningless $\urcorner$ for sentences occurring in the recursion (the recursion is not the same as, but is analogous to, that used for 'true'). By a diagonal construction, we can construct a sentence q such that $q = $ '$\sim \underline{F}'q$''. We can conclude that q is meaningless, because the definition of 'F' provides no way to determine whether it is true or false. But we cannot then go on to use the above definition and conclude that q is true, because q does not occur in the recursion to which the definition applies. On the other hand, if we extend the definition of 'F' as we did above for 'true', we have q and $\sim \underline{F}'q'$, but no paradox ensues.[4]

V

It seems that if we can talk about truth for propositions, then we can construct a completely global truth-predicate for sentences — "expresses a true proposition" — that satisfies the Tarski schema and gives us the Liar paradox back again. But if we cannot talk about truth for propositions, then we cannot say anything about propositions, because all other logical relations and predicates of propositions are defined ultimately (but not exclusively) in terms of truth. And unlike sentences, there is no way to assert a proposition other than saying that it is true. How do we get out of this dilemma? The only solution is to have $\ulcorner E(p, \phi) \urcorner$ meaningless when p is meaningless. Is this solution at all plausible?

4. It is of interest to note that this same sort of solution works for the Grelling paradox (the "heterological" paradox). For a fruitful discussion of this paradox, see Robert L. Martin, "On Grelling's Paradox," _The Philosophical Review_, 77 (1968), 321–31.

Propositions are those things that are (or could be) expressed by meaningful sentences. Given a proposition ϕ, it must be possible to construct a meaningful sentence $\underline{p}$ (possibly by extending the language) such that ϕ is <u>the proposition</u> that $\underline{p}$. Let us abbreviate $\ulcorner$the proposition that $\underline{p}\urcorner$ as $\ulcorner\Pi\underline{p}\urcorner$. We can define a global truth-predicate for propositions easily enough by stipulating: $\ulcorner T(\Pi\underline{p})\urcorner =_{df} \underline{p}$. This is defined for all propositions, because if there is such a proposition as $\Pi\underline{p}$ then $\underline{p}$ is meaningful. Now, how do we define $\ulcorner E('\underline{p}', \phi)\urcorner$? The only way I can see to do this is to stipulate: $\ulcorner E('\underline{p}', \phi)\urcorner =_{df} \ulcorner\phi = \Pi\underline{p}\urcorner$.[5] This is again a type-crossing definition. When it is straightened out and turned into a proper recursive definition (as above for "true"), its range of meaningful applicability only includes meaningful sentences. Thus if $\underline{p}$ is meaningless, it is equally meaningless to say that $\underline{p}$ does or does not express a true proposition. We are not threatened with a recurrence of the Liar paradox.

We have a global truth-predicate for propositions. It seems that we could then use a diagonal construction involving properties and concepts to construct a "Liar proposition" that says of itself that it is not true, and hence we could reconstruct the Liar paradox on the level of propositions. But here we have the option of simply denying that there is any such proposition—a move that is not open to us in the case of the Liar sentence. The conditions under which there exist propositions of certain sorts are not quite so straightforward as the conditions under which certain finite sequences of symbols exist.

The above discussion has the consequence that 'meaningless' cannot be defined, as it frequently is, as 'does not express a proposition'. This is because if a sentence is meaningless, then it is meaningless to say that it does not express a proposition. The traditional definition of 'meaningful' as 'expresses a proposition' belongs to the same sloppy tradition that employed unrestricted type-crossing definitions and got itself involved in the Liar paradox. We also saw that 'meaningless' cannot be defined as 'is neither true nor false'. We seem to be forced to conclude that meaninglessness is a primitive concept—it cannot be defined in terms of other semantical concepts. This is surprising, but I do not think that any strong objection can be made to it.

---

5. This of course presupposes a criterion of identity for propositions, which I am currently unable to supply.

VI

The objection has frequently been made to the language level approach that it makes all self-reference illegitimate, and that this is incorrect. There are quite clear cases of legitimate self-reference in which the self-referential sentences are unequivocally true or false. For example, 'This sentence contains five words' is true. Self-reference only becomes problematic when it involves predicates introduced by type-crossing definitions. And even in that case the self-reference may be legitimate if it can be shown that those predicates can be eliminated.

The above observations also throw some interesting light on Gödel's and Tarski's theorems. First, Tarski's theorem. Given a mathematical theory **T**, if it is strong enough to express the diagonalization function (Martin's norm function), then self-reference is possible in that language. If in addition truth for sentences of **T** were definable in **T**, then semantical self-reference would be possible. Consequently, that language could not contain a completely global truth-concept (satisfying the Tarski schema). But any mathematical predicate definable in **T** will be completely global, so truth for sentences of **T** is not definable in **T**. From this it follows that if derivability is definable in **T**, then derivability cannot be the same thing as truth, and hence **T** is incomplete.

VII

The above solution to the Liar paradox is still in the Chrysippian tradition suggested by Skyrms. However, it differs from Skyrms in that we do not get a completely global truth-predicate satisfying the Tarski schema—only an "almost global" one, defined for all meaningful sentences—and substitutivity of identity is preserved. It is possible to obtain a completely global truth-predicate, but then the Tarski schema fails. I would claim to have given strong reasons for thinking that, because of the meaning of 'true', this is the way things must be. Formally, my solution is almost identical with that presented by Robert Martin. I have given reasons for thinking that 'true' has a limited range of meaningful applicability, and I have argued on the basis of the logic of definitions that there is no logically possible way to extend it to a completely global predicate while preserving the Tarski schema. I differ from Martin only in my treatment of molecular formulas.

A Category Solution to the Liar

by Robert L. Martin

I

Besides disagreement as to the best way to solve the Liar, there is apparently also a more fundamental disagreement as to what constitutes a solution. I see the Liar as raising questions concerning the concepts of sentence (or statement or proposition), truth, negation, reference, etc.; in short, as a problem in the philosophy of language — our language — not <u>primarily</u> as a problem having to do with formalized languages. The problem is, as we all know, that certain assumptions, all of which are to a certain extent plausible, lead to a contradiction. A solution consists in convincing ourselves that at least one of the assumptions that led to the contradiction is after all not so plausible. Obviously if our only move in trying to remove the plausibility of a particular assumption is to treat the argument to contradiction as a <u>reductio,</u> as though it proves that the assumption in question is false, we have failed entirely. What is wanted, ideally, is the uncovering, the making explicit, of some rulelike features of our language which when considered carefully have the effect of blocking at least one of the assumptions of the argument; if not actually showing an assumption to be false, at least casting doubt upon it.

More specifically, I propose to examine the assumption that the Liar sentence has a truth-value, by raising the general question of finding conditions under which sentences have truth-values. The conditions I will discuss have to do with category-correctness. Since I have already argued for this approach in [4] (bracketed numbers indicate references, listed at end of chapter) I will present here: (section II) a summary of the solution in the form of five statements with comments, attempting to deal now with the strengthened form of the Liar along the lines developed briefly in [3], pp. 330, 331; and (section III) a formalized language that incorporates the category solution, and which is demonstrably capable of allowing a good deal of self-reference, including the expression of its own truth-concept.

II

The following five statements together constitute the category solution to the Liar.

    1. Predicates have ranges of applicability (RA's): where an object $\underline{a} \notin RA(\underline{F})$, both $\underline{Fa}$ and $\sim\underline{Fa}$ are without truth-value. Definitions: A sentence of the form $\underline{Fa}$ is <u>semantically</u> <u>correct</u> if and only if $\underline{a} \in RA(\underline{F})$; it is <u>semantically</u> <u>incorrect</u> if and only if $\underline{a} \notin RA(\underline{F})$.

    The negation sign ('$\sim$') stands for choice-negation: $\sim\underline{A}$ is true if and only if $\underline{A}$ is false. We disallow any other kind of negation, negation$_1$ (say, $\underline{Fa}'$ is the negation$_1$ of $\underline{Fa}$), such that $\underline{Fa}'$ is true if and only if $\underline{Fa}$ is false or $a \notin RA(\underline{F})$. (More on this later.)

    2. $RA(T) = RA(\underline{F})$ = set of truth-valued sentences ('T' and 'F' are short for 'is true' and 'is false', respectively). Hence if $\underline{A}$ is truth-valueless so is $T(\underline{A})$ and $F(\underline{A})$, as well as $\sim\underline{A}$; so is $T(\sim\underline{A})$, etc.

    The most likely alternative would be: $RA(T) = RA(\underline{F})$ = set of sentences (i.e. with or without truth-value). The argument for this alternative would be something like the following. Every sentence is exactly one of the three: true, false, neither true nor false. If you say a sentence is true when in fact it is one of the other two possibilities, you have said something false. But this line of argumentation would break down predication restrictions connected with any categories. For example, one might say: a given object is exactly one of the following: red, green, blue, yellow, . . . , none of these. So if I say of some object (say, virtue) that it is red, when in fact it is one of the other possibilities, then I have said something false. (This is not a defense of treating "category mistakes" as without truth-value; it is only a defense, for one who already agrees to that, of restricting the $RA(T)$ to the set of sentences with truth-values.)

    A sentence, as I use the term, is an abstract entity, which may be realized phonically or graphically. A sentence is always a sentence <u>of</u> <u>some</u> <u>language</u>. When I wish to speak of a sentence of English, I will use the quotation-name of the familiar graphic realization of that sentence to do so.

    For many sentences the question of truth and falsity does not arise. There are, to begin with, interrogative, imperative, exclamatory, etc., sentences which are such. Even among the sentences classed grammatically as declarative, there is a subclass to which attention has been drawn by J. L. Austin among others, for which the question of truth and falsity does not arise — examples

may be found in rituals, legal decisions, formal declarations, and
so forth. Consider now a sentence for which the question of truth
and falsity does arise: say, 'The <u>Times</u> was delivered before
breakfast'. It is clear that the question of truth does not arise
relative to the sentence in isolation, but rather to the sentence in
a particular setting. The sentence may be true in one setting,
false in another, and without truth-value in another. Similarly for
sentences like 'All John's children are asleep'.

There is another kind of declarative sentence for which the
question of truth and falsity does not arise; I refer to the so-called
category-mistake sentences, such as 'Virtue is triangular', and
'The number 2 is green'. I will call such sentences semantically
incorrect. They differ fundamentally from some other declarative
sentences that lack truth-value (such as performatives) in being
deviant—they appear in some sense to violate rules of the language,
not simply to lack truth-value. But having said this it is important
to realize that semantically incorrect sentences do have some properties in common with other declarative sentences that lack truth-
value—properties, furthermore, that set them apart from other
deviant·expressions. For example, one can imagine settings in
which semantically incorrect sentences are true or false. Suppose,
for example, that the word 'virtue' in 'Virtue is triangular' is being used referentially to pick out an object in a stylized morality
play. Or again, suppose the expression 'the number 2' is used
referentially to pick out a green numeral. Also, semantically incorrect sentences have important uses (for example in metaphor),
where neither truth nor falsity, but perhaps aptness or inappropri-
ateness, are relevant.

Let us say that semantical incorrectness is a sentence afflic-
tion (common to the language perhaps because of its importance
in metaphor) which can be overcome, as it were (so that truth-
value is restored), in very special settings (as opposed to the very
ordinary settings in which truth-value is restored to sentences
that work sometimes as performatives, or that have subject terms
which are sometimes empty). What sorts of settings are required?
In the example above, where the semantically incorrect sentences
were given settings in which they were true or false, it was necessary to imagine that their subject expressions were used referentially to pick out objects which in fact they misdescribe.

In what follows I argue that the Liar sentence cannot pass the
test for determining semantical correctness. The argument depends on the assumption that the subject expression of the sentence
refers to itself in all settings. This assumption is false, but convenient. A more correct and less convenient approach would be to
operate with a derived notion of semantical incorrectness applying

to sentences in particular settings, and to apply a hypothetical test to the Liar sentence, showing that, in those settings in which it refers to itself, it cannot be shown to be free of this kind of semantical incorrectness. I have tried to work out the details of this approach in [4]. It is more convenient to imagine that one could devise a foolproof self-referential sentence (self-referential in all settings), and to let our version of the Liar stand in for that unwieldy sentence, since most formal treatments of the semantic paradoxes ignore the delicacies of variable settings, and it is useful to be in tune with these treatments.

3. Distinction between reference proper and demonstrative reference: If and only if an expression is used (successfully) to pick out some object, then that object is the demonstrative reference of the expression; if and only if the object is as described by the expression, then the object is the reference proper of the expression.

This distinction is relative to setting—an object is either the reference proper or the demonstrative reference of a definite description of a sentence in a particular setting. But because demonstrative words can be included in descriptions, the importance of variable settings can, for our purpose, be reduced. I will assume that, for example, the expression 'This very 6-word expression' has itself as demonstrative reference and has no reference proper, and this in all settings (the final remarks in the preceding comment apply here). In general I will assume that an expression of the form 'This very expression with property P' has itself (or a longer expression of which it is a part, if there is one) as its demonstrative reference and has itself as its reference proper if and only if it has the property P. That is, I am assuming that the presence of the word 'this very' rules out the possibility of an attributive use of the expressing (if it were used attributively it would have no demonstrative reference).

4. The test for determining whether a self-referential sentence is semantically correct differs from the test for determining whether a non-self-referential sentence is semantically correct in considering the demonstrative reference, not the sense, of the tested sentence. The test for a non-self-referential sentence of the form $\underline{F}a$ is this: does the subject term indicate, on the basis of its sense, an object $\in$ RA($\underline{F}$): $\underline{F}a$ is semantically correct if and only if it does. The test for a self-referential sentence of the form $\underline{F}a$ is this: is the demonstrative reference of the subject term $\in$ RA($\underline{F}$); $\underline{F}a$ is semantically correct if and only if it is.

The reason one tests the semantical correctness of ordinary (non-self-referential) sentences on the basis of the _sense_ of the subject is, I take it, that the subject may not have reference of any sort, and yet it may still be semantically correct. But when we test the semantical correctness of self-referential sentences, it should be clear that we do not need to base our inquiry on the sense of the subject. For with self-referential sentences we have before us, open to inspection, the thing indicated by the subject of the sentence. For any such sentence the (demonstrative) reference of the subject is precisely the expression with which we are dealing. Of course the sort of reference we consider here is the demonstrative reference; we avoid assuming, simply because something is referred to by an expression (for example, 'this very superbly elegant phrase'), that that something is as described.

> 5. Passing the semantical correctness test is a necessary condition for justifiably asserting that a sentence has truth-value. (Cf. 2 above.)

Applying the test to the Liar sentence (a̲: This very sentence is false): For (a̲) to pass the test for semantical correctness, the demonstrative reference of its subject expression must be in the RA of its predicate, 'is false'. To be in that RA an expression must be semantically correct (see 2). The demonstrative reference of the subject is (a̲) itself. So, the test for the semantical correctness of (a̲) requires that we submit (a̲) itself to that test. The infinite regress here rules out (a̲)'s ever passing the test.

Test for Semantical Correctness

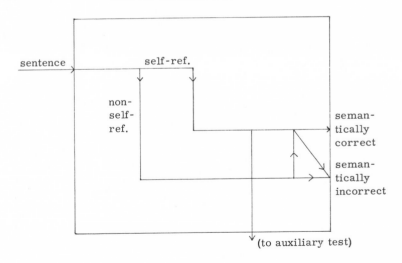

An advantage of this solution is that it does nothing to impugn self-referential sentences in general, even those with semantical predicates such as 'is about', 'is interesting', etc. If we say, for example, that a sentence is about what its subject expression denotes, then it would seem that the RA of 'is about a sentence' is restricted only to the set of sentences (even a semantically incorrect sentence might have a subject expression denoting a sentence); hence the "auxiliary test" (see diagram above) needed in the course of testing 'This very sentence is about a sentence', that is, the test for whether the demonstrative reference of the subject expression belongs to the RA of the predicate, involves submitting the original sentence only to a test of grammaticality, which it clearly passes.

Comment on the Strengthened Liar

The Strengthened Liar can be formulated in either of two ways:

6. This very sentence is not true.
7. This very sentence is either false or without truth-value.

It follows from Statement 1 and the comment made about it that the RA of 'is not true' is the same as the RA of 'is true'. That is, we have disallowed exclusion-negation. So (6) cannot be shown to be semantically correct—it is the same in this respect as (a).

With (7) we must raise the question of determining the RA of a compound predicate—should we take, as the RA of a predicate of the form 'is either P or Q', the union of RA(P) and RA(Q), or the intersection of RA(P) and RA(Q)? I propose that we take the intersection of the two ranges to be the RA of the compound predicate. Therefore, the RA of 'is either false or without truth-value' is the same as that of 'is false'—so (7) fares no better than (a) in our test for semantical correctness. It should be noted that on this view the following inference is not warranted:

S is semantically incorrect
therefore, S is either false or semantically incorrect

since where S is semantically incorrect the premise is true while the conclusion is semantically incorrect.

III

Syntax

We begin with the following primitive symbols:

$$\sim, \text{v}, (,), \text{N}, \text{'},$$

of which only the last two require comment. The last will serve, in pairs, as formal quotation marks, so that an expression within a pair will be understood to be the quotation-name of the enclosed expression. The symbol 'N', here using quotation marks in the metalanguage, which we read 'norm of', serves as a name-forming functor, as specified below.[1] (Intuitively: the norm of

> green

is

> green 'green'.)

We add a countable set of $\underline{n}$-place predicates ($\underline{n}$ = 1, 2 . . .)

$$A, B, C, A_1, \ldots$$

with numerical superscripts to indicate the number of places, a countable set of variables

$$x, y, z, x_1, \ldots$$

and a countable set of individual constants

$$a, b, c, a_1, \ldots$$

Expressions of the language are finite strings of the symbols listed so far. The set of syntactical designators is defined as follows:

D1: For any expression E, $\ulcorner 'E' \urcorner$ is a designator.
D2: For any expression E, if E is a designator, so is $\ulcorner NE \urcorner$.

and the designations of designators as follows:

D3: $\ulcorner 'E' \urcorner$ designates E.
D4: If E_1 designates E_2, then $\ulcorner NE_1 \urcorner$ designates $\ulcorner E_2'E_2' \urcorner$ (i.e. the norm of E_2).

These two syntactic designating devices are not essential to anything of substance in this investigation. What they achieve, aside from simplicity and perspicuousness of notation, could be achieved in the usual semantic way with individual constants. For our purposes, matters are simplified by these devices, since now under any interpretation we will have in the language the name of every expression that occurs in the language. Less obviously, the norm-functor provides us with extensionally self-referential sentences, as will be clear below.

The rest of the syntax of the language is usual. Each atomic formula consists of an $\underline{n}$-place predicate followed by $\underline{n}$ items chosen from among the individual constants, variables, and designators. The set of formulas contains the atomic formulas along with those built up according to the usual rules for negation, dis-

1. See Smullyan, [6]. That paper influenced this one considerably.

junction, and the universal quantifier. Free and bound occurrences of variables are defined in the usual way, and sentences
of the language are formulas in which no variables occur free.
The other connectives and the existential quantifier are introduced by definition in the customary way.

Semantics

The basic idea of the modified semantics is that each interpretation assigns to each predicate of the language not only an extension, but also a range of applicability. In the extension of a predi-
cate $\underline{P}$ are the objects of which $\underline{P}$ is true; in the range of applicability (RA) of $\underline{P}$ are the objects of which $\underline{P}$ is true or false.

An interpretation consists of a nonempty domain D that includes the set of expressions of the language, along with an assignment function : (i) from each term $\underline{t}$ (i.e. individual constant, designator) to $I(\underline{t}) \in D$, i.e. some element of D (where $\underline{t}$ is a designator,
$I(\underline{t})$ is the designation of $\underline{t}$); (ii) from each $\underline{n}$-place predicate $\underline{A}$, to
two sets, one $Ext_I(\underline{A})$, of ordered $\underline{n}$-tuples of elements of D, and the
other, $RA_I(\underline{A})$, not necessarily distinct from $Ext_I(\underline{A})$, also of ordered
$\underline{n}$-tuples of elements of D, and such that $Ext_I(\underline{A}) \subset RA_I(\underline{A})$. We shall
also need the following definition of "$\underline{a}$-variant" for interpretations
I and I', and individual constant $\underline{a}$: I' is an $\underline{a}$-variant of I if and only
if I and I' are identical or I and I' are like except that $I(\underline{a}) \neq I'(\underline{a})$.

Notice that the only formal restriction on the choice of a range
of applicability for a predicate is the obvious one that it include all
objects of which the predicate is true.

We proceed now to the notions of truth and falsity under an interpretation. Truth is handled as usual, since if an object (or an
ordered $\underline{n}$-tuple of objects) is in the extension of a predicate, it is
automatically in its range of applicability; before calling an atomic
sentence false, however, we must be sure that the term is assigned
an object that is at least in the predicate's range of applicability
(or, that the ordered $\underline{n}$-tuple picked out by its terms is one of those
in the predicate's RA). The general definition for atomic sentences,
then, is as follows: an atomic sentence $\underline{A}^{\underline{n}}t_1, t_2, \ldots, t_n$ is true
under I if and only if the ordered $\underline{n}$-tuple $\underline{P}$, that is $\langle I(\underline{t_1}), I(t_2), \ldots,
I(t_n)\rangle \notin Ext_I(\underline{A^{\underline{n}}})$, and false under I if and only if $\underline{P} \in RA_I(\underline{A^{\underline{n}}})$ but
$\underline{P} \notin Ext_I(\underline{A^{\underline{n}}})$. It follows from this definition that there may be atomic
sentences for which no truth-value is defined.

In the treatment of molecular sentences one simple approach
would be to declare any sentence truth-valueless that contains a
truth-valueless molecule.[2] This course seems appropriate for nega-
tions, and I shall adopt it, saying that the negation of a true sentence

---

2. This is the procedure of O'Carroll, [5].

is false, the negation of a false sentence is true, and the negation of a truth-valueless sentence is itself without truth-value. Thus we employ choice-negation. But for disjunctions, on the other hand, it seems more natural to regard the truth of one disjunct as sufficient for the truth of the disjunction (i.e. even if the other is without truth-value),[3] and to regard the falsity of both disjuncts as necessary (and of course sufficient) for the falsity of the disjunction. I should mention that a version of the notion of supervaluation, developed by van Fraassen,[4] can be applied very naturally here with the result that most of the theorems of ordinary two-valued elementary logic come out true under every interpretation of this language. Thus for example, $\ulcorner \underline{A} \vee \sim \underline{A} \urcorner$ is true even under interpretations where $\underline{A}$ has no truth-value. This secures the intuitive point that certain sentences are true solely in virtue of the semantical properties of the connectives and quantifiers. For example, the formal counterparts of 'If virtue is blue, then virtue is blue' and 'If all theories are green, then the theory of relativity is green' are true despite the fact that the atoms involved are without truth-value. For details of this treatment see Appendix B.

Turning now to quantified sentences, a universal quantification $(\underline{x})\underline{A}$ is true under I if and only if its every instantiation is true—more precisely, if and only if $\underline{A}^{\underline{x}}/\underline{a}$ (i.e. the result of replacing all free occurrences of $\underline{x}$ in $\underline{A}$ by occurrences of some individual constant $\underline{a}$ not occuring in $\underline{A}$) is true under all $\underline{a}$-variants of I. To be false, a universal quantification must have at least one instance that is false; that is, $(\underline{x})\underline{A}$ is false under I if and only if $\underline{A}^{\underline{x}}/\underline{a}$ is false under some $\underline{a}$-variant of I. Since the existential quantifier is introduced by definition, its truth and falsity conditions follow naturally. One true instance is necessary and suf-

---

3. In his commentary, "Categories, Negation, and the Liar Paradox," Donnellan shows that I should abandon or at least restrict this principle, and that to do so would accord with a restriction on "compound predicates" proposed in Martin, [3]. The following exception (allowing for cases in which a disjunction is without truth-value even though one disjunct is true) is what is required: <u>A disjunction of one-place atomic sentences with the same term (individual constant, designator) occurring in each atom is without truth-value if either atom is without truth-value.</u> Donnellan's paper and my reply contain a more complete discussion of the matter, including my attempt to rationalize this restriction. One further word here: the precise definition of truth that appears in Appendix B already contains the above restriction as a consequence, though I was unfortunately not aware of this until studying the definition in connection with the repairs made necessary by Donnellan's comments.

4. See [7] and [8].

ficient for the truth of existentially quantified sentences; all instances being false is necessary and sufficient for the falsity of an existentially quantified sentence.

So far we have done nothing more than make the necessary semantic arrangements so that "category-mistake" sentences are treated as neither true nor false. Note that they remain well-formed sentences of the language, in accordance with the fact that category-mistake sentences of English seem to be grammatically correct.[5]

It should also be noted that it is possible for the language to, as it were, ignore the notion of a category-mistake. That is, we allow the possibility that the RA of a given predicate may be identical with the domain of the interpretation. If this is the case under some interpretation I for all predicates of the language, then I is a semantically unrestricted interpretation. It is in effect no different from the usual semantical arrangement, where the notion of RA plays no role. In particular, every sentence is true or false under a semantically-unrestricted interpretation.

But what is the point of the category restrictions? We can see, to put it negatively first, that a semantics that provides only semantically-unrestricted interpretations is incompatible with the aim of fashioning a formalized language capable of expressing its own semantics. For surely part of what it is for a language to be capable of expressing its own semantics is for there to be some interpretation I that assigns to some one-place predicate, say 'T', the set of sentences true under that interpretation. But it is easy to show that no such interpretation is possible, if it is semantically-unrestricted.

5. Something like the approach followed here is mentioned in Bar-Hillel, [1], pp. 30, 31. The approach actually adopted there is to set up rules so that symbol-sequences that correspond to English sentences such as 'Caesar is prime' are not <u>sentences</u> of the formalized language; however, it is remarked there that even if such symbol-sequences are "left in" as sentences, (i) they are "theoretically completely harmless by themselves" (p. 30) and (ii) they can be "immobilized by allowing bilateral reduction sentences" (p. 32; Carnap, [2], pp. 442–43, is cited here). Bar-Hillel's example of "immobilization" indicates that the idea is intuitively akin to our semantical approach: "If one introduces 'is prime' by, say, 'if x is a natural number then x is prime if and only if x is divisible, without remainder, only by itself and by 1', then 'Caesar is prime', though not meaningless, would be paralyzed, and neither truth nor falsehood could be predicated of this sentence, so long, at least, as 'is prime' is not further introduced by other bilateral reduction sentences" (p. 31).

Proof

Suppose there were such a semantically-unrestricted interpretation I; that is, $\text{Ext}_I(T)$ = set of sentences true under I, and $RA_I(T)$ = D. Then consider the sentence

(1) $\sim$TN '$\sim$TN'.

(1) is true under I if and only if

(2) N '$\sim$TN'

designates an expression that is not true under I. However, (2) designates (1), so (1) is true under I if and only if (1) is not true under I. From this follows a contradiction: (1) is both true and not true under I.[6] Hence our original assumption, that there is such an interpretation I, must be given up. The notion of an interpretation with the specifications of I is incoherent.

To put the point of the category restrictions positively, it remains to show that there is a semantically-restricted interpretation under which 'T' plays the role of truth-predicate, and in which the selection of the RA(T) is fairly natural. Notice first of all that if the RA(T) is restricted to the set of sentences of the language for which truth-values are defined, the contradiction just mentioned is blocked. For now the sentence (1) is not assigned either truth-value under the interpretation. To be assigned either it would be necessary that its designator designate a truth-valued sentence, but the designator of (1) designates (1) itself. This circularity blocks the assignment of either truth-value. Of course we could argue more directly to this conclusion: on the assumption that (1) is assigned a truth-value, a contradiction follows. But the important point is that that part of the interpretation which assigns truth-values does not in this case pin either truth-value on (1), so the assumption that

---

6. Notice that the sentence

   $\sim$TN '$\sim$TN'

can be regarded as the formal version of the Grelling as well as the Liar paradox.

   $\sim$TN

is true of exactly the heterological expressions of the language (an expression is heterological if and only if its norm is false), so

   $\sim$TN '$\sim$TN'

asserts, as it were, that 'is heterological' is heterological. See Martin, [3].

there is such an interpretation need not be given up along with the assumption that (1) has a truth-value, as it did with semantically-unrestricted interpretations.

Of course the fact that the contradiction derived earlier is now blocked does not guarantee that no other contradictions are derivable from the assumption that a truth-expressing interpretation of the sort under consideration is possible. The important question here can be formulated as follows. Call I a <u>standard</u> interpretation if it is one in which, for the predicate 'T', $Ext_I(T)$ = set of sentences true under I and in which $RA_I(T)$ = set of sentences which have truth-values under I. Can it be shown that the concept of a standard interpretation is coherent and free of contradiction? The answer is yes; the proof consists in actually producing a standard interpretation and showing that, under it, every sentence of the language comes out exactly one of: true, false, neither true nor false. (See Appendix A for proof.)

Under a standard interpretation, sentences of the language may attribute semantic as well as syntactic properties to other expressions or sets of expressions of the language (other semantic concepts can be defined in terms of truth). Sentences of the language can attribute some properties to themselves—for example, the formal counterpart of 'This sentence is ill-formed',

$$(1) \sim SN \ '\sim SN'$$

where 'S' is assigned the set of well-formed formulas of the language as extension and, most plausibly, the set of expressions as RA, is simply false under that interpretation, since it is clearly well-formed. Consider also the formal counterpart of the sentence, 'This sentence has no truth-value', i.e.

$$(2) \sim VN \ '\sim VN'$$

where $Ext_I(V)$ = set of truth-valued sentences, and $RA_I(V)$ = set of wffs. (2) can be shown to be simply false. First of all, (2) does have some truth-value, since the designation of its designator is a well-formed formula and thus within RA(V). Suppose now that (2) is true. Then it follows that it is without truth-value, which contradicts the assumption. Hence (2) is false.

As a final example of "tolerated" self-reference, note that the formal counterpart of 'This sentence is unprovable', i.e.

$$(3) \sim PN \ '\sim PN'$$

where $Ext_I(P)$ = set of wffs derivable as theorems in the language (assuming that we have introduced sound rules of derivation for this extended predicate calculus), and $RA_I(P)$ = set of wffs, is true under I, and hence unprovable, and this, interestingly enough, even before we have $\underline{\text{specified}}$ the rules. It is, to begin with, true or false. And suppose it is false. Then it is provable, but then, since the rules of derivation are taken to be sound, it follows that it is true under every interpretation, and hence true under I, which contradicts our assumption. Hence (3) is true under I. We have not as yet the full twist of the Gödel result, since the rules in question, with respect to which we have shown that (3) is not provable though true under I, are only rules that pick out sentences true under $\underline{\text{every}}$ interpretation. The point here is that any attempt to devise a special set of axioms and rules, with respect to which a wff is a theorem just in case it is true under I, is from the outset doomed to failure, for we can form a sentence which says of itself, with respect to those axioms and rules, that it is not provable, and show as above that this sentence is true.

IV

It will perhaps already have been noticed that the open sentence '$\sim\underline{Tx}$' is satisfied under a standard interpretation, not by the set of expressions that are not true, but rather by those sentences that are false. That is, '$\sim\underline{Tx}$' is satisfied only by objects for which '$\underline{Tx}$' is false (because of our treatment of negation). The set of nontrue expressions, on the other hand, includes, besides false sentences, sentences without truth-value and nonsentences.

This leads naturally to the idea of assigning the set of nontrue expressions as extension to some other predicate, say 'W'. What should the RA(W) be? Suppose we take the RA(W) to be the set of expressions of the language, as seems perhaps most natural. But this leads to contradiction — a form of what has been called the Strengthened Liar — so we must give up the assumption that there is such an interpretation. To bar the contradiction we must restrict the RA(W) further. Even restricting it to the set of sentences of the language is insufficient to stop the contradiction. What is required is that we restrict it, just as we did the RA(T), to the set of truth-valued sentences. But this restriction violates one of the most intuitively correct provisions of our semantics — the provision that the extension of predicate be included in its range of applicability. If we allowed W as described, it would be true (intuitively speaking) of more things than it applies to, truly or falsely, which is absurd.

Our conclusion is that there can be no interpretation in which the set of expressions that are not true under that interpretation (i.e. the "mixed set," containing nonsentences, truth-valueless sentences, and false sentences) is assigned as extension to a predicate of the language. To put the matter slightly differently, there can be no open atomic sentence of the language which is satisfied by exactly the set of nontrue expressions. The English predicate, 'is not a true sentence', where the 'not' is understood to be a merely "excluding" negation, has no direct counterpart in this language.[7]

Without wishing to minimize this deficiency, I should point out that an open molecular sentence can quite easily be devised which is satisfied by exactly the "mixed" set in question:

$$\sim Tx \; v \sim Vx \; v \sim Sx$$

where $Ext_I(T)$ = set of sentences true under I, $RA_I(T)$ = set of sentences which have a truth-value under I, $Ext_I(V) = RA_I(T)$, $RA_I(V)$ = set of expressions of the language, $Ext_I(S)$ = set of well-formed formulas of the language, $RA_I(S)$ = set of expressions of the language.[8]

The ruling out of a "mixed set" for assignment as extension to a single predicate is reminiscent of Russell's rejection of totalities that contain items of different type. What I must rule out, to put the matter quite generally, is the use in the language of a kind of negation — exclusion negation — that cuts across, or rather ignores, category lines. Let us say that if I understand the assertion '2 is not green' to imply that 2 is actually some other color, then I am taking the negation involved in the assertion to be choice-negation, whereas if I do not understand the assertion to imply any such "other choice" then I am taking the negation to be exclusion-negation. Surely it is on the basis of taking the negation to be of the latter kind that many philosophers declare such sentences to be simply true. I do not wish to speculate on what the word 'not' _really_ means, but only to point out that the intuitive difference between

---

7. Essentially the same situation is reported in O'Carroll, [5], p. 177.

8. Unfortunately, this is false. I have left the paragraph in the paper because it is the subject of some discussion in Donnellan's commentary and in my reply. It can be seen to be false by assigning to the constant 'a' the sentence:

$$\sim Ta \; v \sim Va \; v \sim Sa$$

and noticing that, under the restriction mentioned in n. 3, the sentence is without truth-value. So there is a sentence, the one displayed, which though a member of the "mixed set" does not satisfy

$$\sim Tx \; v \sim Vx \; v \sim Sx$$

even though

$$\sim Va$$

which asserts that the displayed sentence is truth-valueless, is true.

the two kinds of negation is that with the choice-negation one is, as it were, committed to a category-framework, while with the exclusion-negation one ignores, or sees beyond, that framework. To put it crudely, the 'not' tells us to relocate the object referred to by the subject of the sentence, in this case the number 2, moving it outside the class of green things. If one observes category lines and the family relationships among predicates that are part of the category-framework, then the "relocation" puts 2 in the extension of some other predicate that applies to objects of the same category as does 'green', and is at once rejected. However, if one ignores category lines, the relocation simply assigns the number 2 to the extension of some other predicate, and is of course accepted.[9]

Again, all I wish to convey with this vastly oversimplified account of negation is that it is no surprise that if one were to take one's categories very seriously, the exclusion variety of negation would have to go. My idea about the semantical paradoxes is that they can be blamed on our not taking the category-framework seriously enough. Now in formalizing enough of the category-framework to stop the paradoxes and thus allow semantic inclusion, we find that exclusion-negation must be eschewed.

This applies to our discussion of 'not true' as follows. It is essential to my account that a category-distinction be drawn between sentences that are true or false and those that are neither. This is reflected in the fact that the range of applicability of 'is true' and 'is false' is restricted to truth-valued sentences, while the RA of 'has a truth-value' and 'is without truth-value' is restricted only to the set of expressions of the language. The 'not' as expressed by the negation sign of the formalized language is clearly choice-negation: '∼A' is true if and only if 'A' is false, i.e. belongs to the extension of its category-mate predicate. The sense of 'not true' we have tried to incorporate was one in which

9. I have assumed throughout that the RA of the predicate 'is green' is restricted, perhaps to the set of physical objects, in such a way that numbers are excluded. As far as the formalized language is concerned, one could introduce a predicate for 'is green' with whatever RA one chose (allowing the possibility of regarding the predicate as applicable to everything in the domain)—that is, there are interpretations under which the formal counterpart of '2 is not green' would be true. The most one can say is that if in given circumstances the predicate 'is green' has associated with it the restricted RA that it seems to in most ordinary contexts, and if further choice-negation is employed, then '2 is not green' is without truth-value.

the category difference just mentioned was ignored. And this exclusion-negation, applied here to the semantically crucial concept of truth, had to be ruled out of the formalized language.

That something which is to some extent natural must be given up in a treatment of the semantic paradoxes seems very clear; they are, to use Quine's terminology, genuine antinomies, rather than viridical paradoxes, precisely because they can be formulated in a way in which all the necessary assumptions are to some extent plausible. It is in this light that I think one should view the loss of exclusion-negation in the formalized langue presented above as the actual cash cost of buying a category-framework in which the paradoxes do not arise.

To end on an appropriately self-referential note: it is clear that at times in this paper I have not only mentioned but also used exclusion-negation. This suggests the question: is it possible to set up a theory of categories without the use of the very category-free negation that led to the trouble in the first place. This question is related to the one that hounded Russell's theory of types: is it possible to propound the theory without thereby violating it. I need to answer this question as well as to examine even more fundamental questions concerning the relationship between a proposed conceptual reform and the framework in which it is recommended; but consideration of these matters obviously lies beyond the scope of this paper.

Appendix A. Proof that There Are Standard Interpretations

We specify an interpretation I as follows:

Domain = $M \cup L$ (M = set of positive integers; L = set of expressions of the language.)

The extension of each $\underline{n}$-place predicate (for any $\underline{n}$) except 'T^1' (henceforth the superscript is omitted) is a set of ordered $\underline{n}$-tuples of elements of M; the RA of each $\underline{n}$-place predicate except 'T' is the set of all ordered $\underline{n}$-tuples of elements of M. Each individual constant denotes itself. $RA_I(T)$ = set of sentences for which truth-values are defined under I.

The $Ext_I(T)$ is given below, with the help of the following: I adopt the supervaluation technique explained in Appendix B and assume that we have a sound and complete set of rules for our extended predicate calculus. On the basis of these rules we have the usual notion of <u>theorem</u> (sentence derivable from the empty set of sentences). We let 'TH' denote the set of theorems, and for any set S of sentences, we let 'Con(S)' denote the set of sentences that are derivable from S (S $\subset$ Con(S)).

$\text{Ext}_I(T)$ = the smallest set X such that
1. TH $\subset$ X
2. for any designator D (with designation d), if d ϵ X, then $\ulcorner TD \urcorner \epsilon$ X
3. for any designator D (with designation d), if $\ulcorner \sim d \urcorner \epsilon$ X, then $\ulcorner \sim TD \urcorner \epsilon$ X
4. Con (X) $\subset$ X.

Comments

The above interpretation has been designed to afford maximum simplicity in allowing us to show that no contradiction arises from allowing the language the expression of its own truth-concept. In particular, it will be noted that every atomic sentence beginning with any predicate other than 'T' lacks truth-value under I, since its terms denote expressions of the language while the RA of its predicate is restricted to sets of numbers.

Metatheorem: For any sentence $\underline{A}$, (1) $\underline{A}$ is exactly one of the following under I: true, false, without truth-value (N), and (2) $\underline{A} \epsilon \text{Ext}_I(T)$ if and only if $\underline{A}$ is true under I (that is, I is a standard interpretation of the language).

Proof: We assign a degree (0, 1, 2, . . .) to every sentence $\underline{A}$, and prove by mathematical induction on the degree of $\underline{A}$ that (1) and (2) hold for every sentence $\underline{A}$.

The degree of $\underline{A}$:

D1: Atomic sentences none of whose terms designates a sentence are of degree 0.

D2: For any sentence $\underline{A}$ of degree $\underline{n}$ and term $\underline{t_i}$, if $I(\underline{t_i}) = \underline{A}$, then the sentences $\underline{B}(t_i)$ (one of whose terms is $\underline{t_i}$, where there is no term $\underline{t_j}$ in $\underline{B}$, $I(\underline{t_j}) = \underline{C}$, $\underline{C}$ of degree greater than $\underline{n}$) and $\sim\underline{A}$ are of degree $\underline{n}+1$. In other words, the degree of $\underline{B}$ is 1 greater than that of the sentence of highest degree "mentioned" by a term in $\underline{B}$; the degree of the negation of a sentence is 1 greater than that of the sentence negated.

D3: If the sentences $\underline{X}$ and $\underline{Y}$ are of degrees $\underline{n_1}$ and $\underline{n_2}$, respectively, then $\ulcorner \underline{X} \text{ v } \underline{Y} \urcorner$ is of degree $\underline{n_1}+\underline{n_2}+1$.

D4: For any sentence $\underline{A}(\underline{t})$, one of whose terms is $\underline{t}$, of degree $\underline{n}$, $\ulcorner (\underline{x})\underline{A}(\underline{x}) \urcorner$ is of degree $\underline{n}+1$ (where $\underline{A}(\underline{x})$ is the result of replacing all occurrences of $\underline{t}$ in $\underline{A}$ by occurrences of $\underline{x}$).

Before proceeding we note that the following are consequences of the above characterization of $\text{Ext}_I(T)$ and the definition of 'true under an interpretation I' given in Appendix B.

1. If $\underline{A} = \underline{B}t_1, t_2 \ldots t_n$ (where $\underline{B}$ is any predicate other than 'T'), and for some $\overline{t_i}$, $I(t_i)$ is a sentence, then $\underline{A} \notin \text{Ext}_I(T)$.
2. If $\underline{A} = \ulcorner T t \urcorner$, where $\overline{I(t)} \in \text{Ext}_I(T)$, then $\underline{A} \in \text{Ext}(T)$.
3. If $\underline{A} = \ulcorner T t \urcorner$, where $I(t) \notin \text{Ext}_I(T)$, then $\underline{x} \notin \text{Ext}_I(T)$.
4. If $\underline{A} = \ulcorner {\sim}\underline{B} \urcorner$, $\underline{B} \in \text{Ext}_I(T)$, then $\underline{A} \notin \text{Ext}_I(T)$.
5. If $\underline{A} \quad \ulcorner {\sim}\underline{B} \urcorner$, $\underline{B} \notin \text{Ext}_I(T)$ and $\underline{B}$ is N (without truth-value), then $\underline{A} \notin \text{Ext}_I(T)$.
6. If $\underline{A} = \ulcorner \underline{B} \vee \underline{C} \urcorner$, where at least one of $\underline{B}, \underline{C} \in \text{Ext}_I(T)$, then $\underline{A} \in \text{Ext}_I(T)$.
7. If $\underline{A} = \ulcorner \underline{B} \vee \underline{C} \urcorner$, where both $\underline{B}$ and $\underline{C}$ are false under I, then $\underline{A} \notin \text{Ext}_I(T)$.
8. If $\underline{A} = \ulcorner \underline{B} \vee \underline{C} \urcorner$, where one of $\underline{B}, \underline{C}$ is N, the other false, $\underline{A} \notin \text{Ext}_I(T)$.
9. If $\underline{A} = (x)\underline{B}$, for variable $\underline{x}$ and formula $\underline{B}$, and $\underline{A}^{\underline{x}}/\underline{a}$ is true under every $\underline{a}$-variant of I, then $\underline{A} \in \text{Ext}_I(T)$.
10. If $\underline{A} = (x)\underline{B}$ for variable $\underline{x}$ and formula $\underline{B}$, and $\underline{A}^{\underline{x}}/\underline{a}$ is false under some $\underline{a}$-variant of $\underline{A}$, then $\underline{A} \notin \text{Ext}_I(T)$.
11. If $\underline{A} = (x)\underline{B}$, for variable $\underline{x}$ and formula $\underline{B}$, and $\underline{A}^{\underline{x}}/\underline{a}$ is N under some $\underline{a}$-variant of I, then $\underline{A} \notin \text{Ext}_I(T)$.

Now for the induction:

I. The properties 1 and 2 of the Metatheorem hold for sentences of degree 0; all are N and $\notin \text{Ext}_I(T)$.

II. Suppose both 1 and 2 hold for all sentences of degree $< \underline{n}$. Then both hold for all sentences of degree $\underline{n}$.

Cases

1. $A = \underline{B}t_1, t_2 \ldots tk$, where $\underline{B}$ is a predicate other than "T", and where $I(t_i)$ is a sentence. Then $\underline{A}$ is N and $\notin \text{Ext}_I(T)$.
2. $\underline{A} = \ulcorner T t \urcorner$ where $I(t)$ is some sentence. Then $\underline{A}$ is true if $I(t)$ is true, false if $I(t)$ is false, and N if $I(t)$ is N; $\underline{A}$ is true if and only if $\underline{A} \in \text{Ext}_I(T)$ (see 2, 3 above).
3. $\underline{A} = \ulcorner {\sim}\underline{B} \urcorner$, where $\underline{B}$ is of degree $\underline{n}-1$. $\underline{B}$ is by hypothesis exactly one of true, false, N. If true, $\underline{A}$ is false, if false $\underline{A}$ is true, if N $\underline{A}$ is N (from definition of truth). Suppose $\underline{B}$ is true. Then $\underline{B} \in \text{Ext}_I(T)$ by hypothesis, and hence $\underline{A} \notin \text{Ext}_I(T)$. (Cf. 4). If $\underline{B}$ is N, then $\underline{B} \notin \text{Ext}_I(T)$, by hypothesis, and hence $\underline{A} \notin \text{Ext}_I(T)$. (Cf. 5). If $\underline{B}$ is false, then there are four possibilities.
   - (3a) $\underline{B}$ is atomic, $\underline{B} = \ulcorner T\underline{D} \urcorner$ where d is false;
   - (3b) $\underline{B} = {\sim}\underline{C}$ where $\underline{C}$ is true;
   - (3c) $\underline{B} = \ulcorner \underline{C} \vee \underline{D} \urcorner$ where both $\underline{C}$ and $\underline{D}$ are false;
   - (3d) $\underline{B} = \ulcorner (x)\underline{C} \urcorner$ where $\underline{C}^{\underline{x}}/\underline{a}$ is false under some $\underline{a}$-variant of I.

If (3a), then $\ulcorner \sim d \urcorner$ is of degree $\underline{n}-1$ and true ($\underline{B}$ is of degree $\underline{n}-1$, so d is of degree $\underline{n}-2$, so $\ulcorner \sim d \urcorner$ is of degree $\underline{n}-1$; the negation of a false sentence is true). Then by hypothesis, $\ulcorner \sim d \urcorner \in \text{Ext}_I(T)$, hence $\underline{A}$ (i.e. $\ulcorner \sim T\underline{D} \urcorner$) $\in \text{Ext}_I(T)$ (by clause 3 of the definition of $\text{Ext}_I(T)$).

If (3b), then since $\underline{C}$ is true and of degree $\underline{n}-2$, $\underline{C} \in \text{Ext}_I(T)$. Hence $\underline{A}$ (i.e. $\ulcorner \sim\sim C \urcorner$) $\in \text{Ext}_I(T)$ (by clause 4 of the definition of $\text{Ext}_I(T)$).

If (3c), then both $\ulcorner \sim\underline{C} \urcorner$ and $\ulcorner \sim\underline{D} \urcorner$ are true and $\in \text{Ext}_I$ (T), since both have degree $< \underline{n}$. Then $\underline{A}$ (i.e. $\sim(\underline{C} \vee \underline{D})$) $\in \text{Ext}_I(T)$ (by clause 4 of the definition of $\text{Ext}_I(T)$).

If (3d), then $\sim\underline{C}^{\underline{x}}/a$ is of degree $\underline{n}-1$ and true under some $\underline{a}$-variant of I. Let $\underline{b}$ be a constant not in $\underline{C}$ and such that $\sim\underline{C}^{\underline{x}}/b$ is true under I. Then $\ulcorner \sim\underline{C}^{\underline{x}}/\underline{b} \urcorner \in \text{Ext}_I(T)$, and hence $\underline{A}$ (i.e. $\sim(\underline{x})\underline{C}x$) $\in \text{Ext}_I(T)$ (by clause 4 of the definition of $\text{Ext}_I(T)$).

4. $\underline{A} = \ulcorner \underline{B} \vee \underline{C} \urcorner$, where the degree $(\underline{B})$ + degree $(\underline{C}) = \underline{n}-1$. $\underline{B}$ and $\underline{C}$ are both by hypothesis exactly one of true, false, N. $\underline{A}$ is true if one is true, false if both are false, and N otherwise, and $\underline{A} \in \text{Ext}_I(T)$ if and only if $\underline{A}$ is true (Cf. 6, 7, 8 above).

5. $\underline{A} = (\underline{x})\underline{B}$, for formula $\underline{B}$, where $\underline{B}^{\underline{x}}/t$, for any term $\underline{t}$, is of degree $\underline{n}-1$. (1) and (2) hold for $\underline{A}$ (Cf. 9, 10, 11).

Appendix B. Supervaluations

Definition: A sentence $\underline{A}$ is true (false) under an interpretation I if and only if the supervaluation of $\underline{A}$ under I is T (F).

Supervaluation under I: Assign T (F) to $\underline{A}$ if and only if it has valuations under I and every valuation of $\underline{A}$ under I yields T (F).

Valuation under I:
(i) If $\underline{A} = \underline{A}^{\underline{n}}t_1, t_2, t_3, \ldots t_n$, then give T to $\underline{A}$ if the ordered $\underline{n}$-tuple $\underline{P}$, that is $\langle I(\underline{t_1}), I(\underline{t_2}), \ldots I(\underline{t_n}) \rangle \in \text{Ext}_I(\underline{A}^{\underline{n}})$, and F to $\underline{A}$ if P $\in \text{RA}_I(\underline{A}^{\underline{n}})$ but P $\notin \text{Ext}_I(\underline{A}^{\underline{n}})$.
(ii) If $\underline{A} = (\underline{x})\underline{B}$, for variable $\underline{x}$ and formula $\underline{B}$, then give T to $\underline{A}$ if $\underline{B}^{\underline{x}}/a$ is true under every $\underline{a}$-variant of I, and F to $\underline{A}$ if $\underline{B}^{\underline{x}}/a$ is false under some $\underline{a}$-variant of I.
(iii) If $\underline{A} = \sim\underline{B}$ or $\underline{A} = (\underline{B} \vee \underline{C})$, for sentences $\underline{B}$ and $\underline{C}$, then: (a) assign T or F to every truth-functional part of $\underline{A}$ in accordance with (i) and (ii) above. Where (i) and (ii) do not specify, the assignment is arbitrary except that whatever interpretation changes are presupposed by one assignment are kept in force throughout that valuation (it follows that each occurrence of a given truth-functional part

is assigned the same truth-value throughout each valuation);[10] (b) assign T or F to $\underline{A}$ on the basis of the standard (two-valued) truth-table computation.

It may be instructive to consider an example. Take the sentence $\underline{A}$:

(x) (Fx v ~Fx).

This is true under I if and only if its supervaluation under I is T. Its supervaluation is T if and only if its every valuation under I yields T. Here clause (ii) above is applicable. We see that $\underline{A}$ has the valuation T under I if and only if 'Fa v~Fa' is true under every $\underline{a}$-variant of I. And it is easy to see that 'Fa v ~Fa' is true under every $\underline{a}$-variant of I (in other words, no matter what I($\underline{a}$) is taken to be). 'Fa v ~Fa' is true under I if and only if its supervaluation under I is T, i.e. if and only if its every valuation under I assigns it T. Clause (iii) is now applicable and it is obvious that, no matter whether Fa gets an assignment of T or F or not, the sentence 'Fa v ~Fa' is assigned T for its every valuation. Hence, $\underline{A}$ is true under I.

For a slightly more complex example consider sentence $\underline{B}$:

~(x)Fx v ~(x)~Fx

which is, by definition, '(x)Fx $\supset$ ($\exists$x)Fx'. $\underline{B}$ is true under an interpretation I if and only if its supervaluation under I is true, that is, if and only if it is assigned T by all possible valuations. Clause (iii) of the valuation rule is initially applicable, and according to it we assign T or F to '(x)Fx' and '(x)~Fx' in accordance with clause (ii). There are six possibilities here, depending on the nature of the interpretation (i.e. the domain D, the RA(F), the Ext(F)), and three impossibilities. The possibilities are:

---

10. It follows further that it will be impossible to produce a valuation for some molecular sentences —so these will have no truth-value. Consider, for example, 'Aa v Ba' where I(a) $\in$ Ext(A) but I(a)$\notin$RA(B), and RA(A)$\cap$RA(B) = Λ. From clause (i) 'Aa' gets T and 'Ba' gets no assignment. Then under (iii) we attempt first to assign T and then F to 'Ba'. The interpretation change which must be understood for assigning T to 'Ba' is that 'a' is given another assignment, I'(a), such that I'(a)$\in$Ext(b). But we cannot keep this interpretation change in force throughout the valuation, since under it the first disjunct 'Aa' loses its T assignment. Similarly, it is impossible to assign F to 'Ba', keeping in force the interpretation changes presupposed.

	(x)Fx	(x)~Fx
(1)	F	F
(2)	T	F
(3)	F	T
(4)	–	F
(5)	F	–
(6)	–	–

For example, (1) holds for interpretations where some elements of D are in Ext(F) and there are elements in RA(F) that are not in Ext(F); (4) holds for interpretations that are like those just mentioned, except that everything in RA(F) is in Ext(F); (5) holds for interpretations where some but not all elements of D belong to RA(F) but none to Ext(F); (6) holds for interpretations where RA(F) is empty.

The impossibilities are:

	(x)Fx	(x)~Fx
(7)	T	T
(8)	T	–
(9)	–	T

For there is no interpretation, (7), in which everything has and lacks property F; (8) for every interpretation in which '(x)Fa' is T, one instance falsifies '(x)~Fx'; (9) for any interpretation in which (x)~Fx is T, one instance falsifies (x)Fx.

The second part of clause (iii) now instructs us to assign T and F arbitrarily to the truth-functional parts of $\underline{B}$ that are as yet unspecified (with the restriction noted there), and then to compute the truth-value of $\underline{B}$ in the usual way. For interpretations yielding case (1) assignments, $\underline{B}$ comes out T; similarly for interpretations yielding case (2) and (3) assignments, since in each case one truth-functional part is F. For interpretations yielding case (4) and (5) assignments, there are two possible valuations each for $\underline{B}$, but both are T.

	~(x)Fx	v ~(x)~Fx
(4a)	F T	T T F
(4b)	T F	T T F
(5a)	T F	T F T
(5b)	T F	T T F

For interpretations yielding case (6) assignments, the restriction on arbitrary assignments comes into play. For suppose we assign T to '(x)Fx'. Our list of impossible assignments makes it clear that any interpretation that gives T to '(x)Fx' gives F to '(x)~Fx'. So keeping the interpretation changes presupposed by the assignment of T to '(x)Fx' throughout the valuation, we must give F to '(x)∼Fx'. However, if we assign F to '(x)Fx', no assignment is fixed for '(x)∼Fx'. Hence case (6) splits into 3 valuations:

	∼(x)Fx	v ∼(x)∼Fx
(6a)	F T	T T F
(6b)	T F	T F T
(6c)	T F	T T F

We may conclude that, for every possible interpretation, $\underline{B}$ is given T by its supervaluation, since each valuation of every interpretation yields T. That is to say, $\underline{B}$ is true under every interpretation.

References

[1] Bar-Hillel, Y., "On Syntactic Categories," The Journal of Symbolic Logic, 15 (1950), 1–16. Reprinted in Bar-Hillel, Language and Information, Reading, Mass., Addison-Wesley Publishing Co., 1964. Page references are to this reprinting.

[2] Carnap, R., "Testability and Meaning," Philosophy of Science, 3 (1936), 419–71; 4 (1937), 1–40.

[3] Martin, R. L., "On Grelling's Paradox," The Philosophical Review, 77 (1968), 321–31.

[4] Martin, R. L., "Toward a Solution to the Liar Paradox," The Philosophical Review, 76 (1967), 279–311.

[5] O'Carroll, M. J., "A Three-Valued, Non-levelled Logic Consistent for All Self-Reference," Logique et Analyse, 38 (1967), 173–78.

[6] Smullyan, R. M., "Languages in which Self-Reference Is Possible," Journal of Symbolic Logic, 22 (1957), 55–67.

[7] van Fraassen, B., "Singular Terms, Truth-Value Gaps, and Free Logic," The Journal of Philosophy, 63 (1966), 481–95.

[8] van Fraassen, B., "The Completeness of Free Logic," Zeitschrift für mathematische Logik und Grundlagen der Mathematik, 12 (1966), 219–34.

Categories, Negation, and the Liar Paradox

by Keith S. Donnellan

In earlier papers Martin made interesting use of the notion of categories to propose solutions for the Grelling paradox and for the (standard version of the) Liar.[1] The question is whether his approach can handle the Strengthened Liar paradox. His present paper attempts to show that it can. I think he runs into difficulties at various points. But whether or not he has resources for overcoming them, his paper raises important issues about the possibility of category-distinctions, about the necessity, if any, for two modes of negation, and about the connection between these two well-known problems.

In several papers in this volume, two kinds of negation have been mentioned, "choice" negation and "exclusion" negation. The distinction is an old one, going back to Aristotle and has been marked by various names ("exclusion" negation has been called "infinite" negation and "weak" negation). To block the Strengthened Liar, Martin proposes that we eschew exclusion negation (for a start). There is, perhaps, something ironic about this, since he invokes the philosophical notion of category differences as the key to the solution of the paradoxes and yet that notion is probably the main prop for the belief that there is more than one way to negate a proposition.

It turns out, however, that abandoning exclusion negation does not suffice, by itself, to block the Strengthened Liar. One must also, as Martin does, restrict the range of applicability of the predicates, 'is true' and 'is false'. But even that, I think, is not enough. A decision has also to be made about how to treat molecular or compound sentences and molecular or compound predicates. And here, I believe, Martin's treatment involves him in an inconsistency. I will try to point out where I think it lies, though I think it is an inconsistency he can avoid by local repairs.

1. Robert L. Martin, "Toward a Solution to the Liar Paradox," The Philosophical Review, 76 (1967), 279–311, and "On Grelling's Paradox," The Philosophical Review, 77 (1968), 321–31.

But there seems to be a more fundamental difficulty in Martin's approach. To countenance categories is to believe that particular predicates yield true or false sentences only when applied to some restricted range of subjects and that, if applied to subjects outside this range, the resulting sentence has no truth-value.[2] Thus we might say that the predicate 'is red' when applied to a physical object, i.e. affixed to a term referring to a physical object, yields a sentence that is either true or false, but that when it is applied to, say, a number, the result has no truth-value. We can say that the "range of applicability," to use Martin's terminology, of the predicate 'is red' includes physical objects, but not numbers.

A question arises, however, about what to do about negation. On the one hand if a sentence, '$\underline{F}a$', has no truth-value, we are inclined to say that its negation has none either. Or to put it the other way, if '$\underline{F}a$' is true, then 'not-$\underline{F}a$' is false, and vice versa. Given that predicates have restricted ranges of application, this would be to view the negation of a sentence as choice negation. So if 'The number 3 is red' has no truth-value, neither on this account does its negation, 'It is not the case that the number 3 is red'.

But after all, for whatever reason, the predicate 'is red' does not apply correctly to the number 3; being red is not a property of the number 3. It looks as though we ought to be able to express this by saying that it is <u>not</u> the case that the number 3 is red. But this seems to introduce another kind of negation, excluding negation, for here if '$\underline{F}a$' has no truth-value, then 'not-$\underline{F}a$' is not without truth-value: in fact it is true.

I believe that this is at least one of the considerations philosophers have used for introducing two kinds of negation. It allows them to say that, in one sense of negation, 'It is not the case that the number 3 is red' has no truth-value, but that in another sense of negation it is true. In this way we can accommodate both of the things we are inclined to say about the situation where a predicate is being used in conjunction with a subject to which it cannot, because of category restrictions, apply.

---

2. Throughout I talk of <u>sentences</u> possessing truth or falsity to conform to Martin's usage. I don't think it matters, regarding what I say (and perhaps what he says), that I, for one, would be dubious that sentences rather than, say, propositions are the things that have truth-value. I believe that, for example, 'proposition' can be substituted throughout without altering the argument. The essential point is that there is supposed to be a class of things, whatever they are, that are either true, false, or without truth-value.

There is, however, a way of doing this without introducing two kinds of negation. We could hold that there is just one kind of negation, choice-negation, and that if 'Fa' has no truth-value, neither does 'not-Fa'. But where a predicate does not apply to a subject because it lies outside the predicate's range of application, we can express this fact by saying, for example, 'It is not true that the number three is red'. Or, if we want to attach truth to sentences, 'The sentence 'The number 3 is red' is not true'. When we are inclined to say that after all it is not the case that the number 3 is red, seeming to use excluding negation, what we mean is that it is not true that the number 3 is red, where the negation applies to the predicate 'is true' and not to the predicate 'is red'. And there is so far no reason to suppose that the negation is different, for now the question becomes, what is the range of application of the predicate, 'is true'? If the sentence 'The number 3 is red' is within that range, even though it has no truth-value, then we can construe the negation as choice-negation and we have not introduced a new kind of negation.

There may be other reasons why one might wish to speak of two kinds of negation, but the reason that arises out of the philosophical notion of categories I just mentioned does not in the end seem a good one so long as the range of application of 'is true' (and 'is false' as well, of course) extends to sentences without truth-value.

To return to Martin's treatment of the Strengthened Liar, it turns out that since having only one kind of negation, choice-negation, does not suffice to solve the paradox, he must also limit the range of application of the predicates, 'is true' and 'is false', to those sentences that have a truth-value. (He does this in his paper and in a moment I will try to show why it is necessary for him to do it.)

The point I want to make here is that Martin seems to me to leave himself no way of _saying_ what, after all, constitutes the central idea in the theory of category differences: that when a particular predicate is applied to a subject outside the range of application of the predicate, the result is not true and it is not false. If he had two kinds of negation, he could express this by 'It is not the case that _Fa_', where the negation is exclusion negation. But he does not allow that. If the range of application of the predicate, 'is true', were to extend to those sentences that have no truth-value, he could express it by 'It is not true that _Fa_' or by ''_Fa_' is not true'. But he cannot allow that either.

So we are left with a somewhat odd situation. The attempt at solving the Strengthened Liar demands that there be a class of things — Martin takes it to be the class of sentences, but it would not matter if it were thought of as propositions or statements or whatever—which divides into three mutually exclusive proper subsets: those that are true, those that are false, and the remainder. And yet the apparatus for solving the Strengthened Liar does not allow one to say in all cases that a member of the genus class is not a member of one of the subclasses, even though the subclasses are mutually exclusive. If a sentence, or whatever, is a member of the "remainder," as I have called it, one cannot say that it is not a member of the subclass of true sentences, or of false sentences. Yet it is important that, after all, we know just this about certain sentences. I find this perhaps as great a paradox as the Strengthened Liar.

II

Turning now to the mechanics of Martin's attempt at solving the Strengthened Liar, does he succeed, even if at some cost? The simple Liar paradox using the sentence, 'This very sentence is false', can be blocked by any view a consequence of which is that sentences of that kind have no truth-value. The Strengthened Liar attempts to rejuvenate the paradox by using self-referential sentences that say of themselves that either they are false _or_ they have no truth-value. This is supposed to have the result that declaring these sentences to have no truth-value will be of no avail because this will entail that what they say about themselves is after all true. Any theory that totally prescribes self-reference, however, has no difficulty with the Strengthened Liar. The sentences involved have no truth-value and that is an end to the matter. The fact they _seem_ to say of themselves something true cuts no ice because, since they involve self-reference, they do not succeed in saying anything about themselves at all. But it is Martin's aim to solve the paradoxes while preserving the _general_ possibility of self-reference (for, I think, good reasons). The Strengthened Liar thus poses a real difficulty for him.

There are several kinds of sentences that can be used to generate the Strengthened Liar, and although in some sense they say the same thing (if they say anything at all) they say it in somewhat different ways.

The following are some of the sentences that can be used in the Strengthened Liar:

> (1) This very sentence is not true. (Where being not true does not entail being false, but allows for the possibility of having no truth-value.)
> (2) This very sentence has the property W. (Where the extension of the artificial predicate 'W' is the set of sentences that are either false or without truth-value.)

(3) This very sentence is either false or without truth-value.

Martin would say that the negation in (1), the word 'not', must have the force of <u>exclusion</u> negation rather than <u>choice</u>-negation. To say that <u>a</u> is not <u>F</u> where 'not' has the force of <u>exclusion</u> negation is simply to say that <u>a</u> is not part of the extension of <u>F</u>, whereas to say it with the force of <u>choice</u>-negation is not only to say this but also to say that <u>a</u> is part of the extension of a member of some range of predicates other than <u>F</u>. What that range is will depend presumably upon what <u>F</u> is (i.e. what category it belongs to). Thus '<u>a</u> is not red' using exclusion negation would be true both if <u>a</u> is yellow and if <u>a</u> is not the <u>sort</u> of thing (the number 2) that could have a color. Whereas using choice-negation this would be true only if <u>a</u> has some other color (or, at least, could have some other color).

Now (1) interpreted as using exclusion negation does generate the Strengthened Liar unless measures are taken against it. And therefore Martin bans the notion of exclusion-negation from his scheme of things. But the interesting thing is that even if (1) is read as involving choice-negation the paradox can still be gotten unless other measures are taken. I will return to this point later.

Sentence (2) does not on the surface seem to raise any issues about negation at all, although, of course, we used negation in specifying the extension of its predicate. Martin legislates against the predicate, the artificial predicate 'W' (though it seemed to me a bit <u>ad hoc</u> to do so). But, as we shall see, this proscription can only be made to stick if several other measures are taken.

Why on Martin's view does (3) not produce the Strengthened Liar? Having ruled out the predicate 'W' as exemplified in sentence (2) he goes on to say, "I should point out that an open molecular sentence can quite easily be devised which is satisfied by exactly the 'mixed' set in question,"[3] where he means, by the "mixed" set, the set of all those strings of symbols that do not form true sentences. The molecular sentence he gives is:

$$\sim Tx \text{ v} \sim Vx \text{ v} \sim Sx,$$

where we can read 'T' as 'is true', 'V' as 'has a truth-value', and 'S' as 'is a well-formed sentence'. If Martin admits that this open molecular sentence has as its extension the "mixed set," then its extension is the same as that of the predicate 'W', which was excluded. But it looks like there is no way to prevent 'W' from being reintroduced by definition—'W_x' $=_{df}$ '$\sim Tx$ v $\sim Vx$ v $\sim Sx$'.

---

3. "A Category Solution to the Liar," this volume, p. 104.

Be that as it may the open sentence can be used to generate the Strengthened Liar even if the negation sign occurring in it is read as representing choice-negation, showing that eliminating exclusion negation has not by itself done away with the paradox:

(4) This very sentence is a member of the extension of the open sentence, '$\sim Tx \; v \sim Vx \; v \sim Sx$.'

(4) can be used to generate the paradox. Also, since in Martin's formal system individual constants can, under an interpretation, be the names of sentences in which they occur (to allow for the general possibility of self-reference), the following sentence gives us the Strengthened Liar:

(5) $\sim Ta \; v \sim Va \sim Sa,$

where 'a' is the name of sentence (5).

The fact that the negation in sentence (5) is to be read as choice-negation doesn't affect things at all. Counting it as choice-negation merely means that if 'Ta' has no truth-value, then the first disjunct of (5) has no truth-value, and if 'Va' has no truth-value, the second disjunct has no truth-value, and similarly for the third. Since (5) is conceded to be well-formed, the third disjunct must in any case be false. But then we can argue along the familiar lines that if (5) is true, there is no true disjunct in it and hence it must be false; that if it is false then 'Ta' must be false and the first disjunct, '$\sim Ta$', true and hence the whole sentence is true; and finally if it has no truth-value 'Va' must be false and the second disjunct, '$\sim Va$', true and hence it does have a truth-value.

In fact eliminating exclusion-negation in favor of choice-negation does not even serve to block the paradox utilizing sentence (1), 'This very sentence is not true'. Everything depends upon what we take the range of application of 'is true' to be. If it includes sentences that have no truth-value as well as those that do, then even though 'not' is construed as choice-negation, the supposition that the sentence has no truth-value entails that it is after all true.

What follows from this is that not only must Martin prevent us from using exclusion-negation, but he must also, as a separate prohibition, restrict the range of application of the predicates 'is true' and 'is false' to those sentences that have truth-value.

But when we turn again to (5), even that is not enough. For (5) is a disjunction and if, as Martin does, we adopt the rule that it is sufficient for the truth of a disjunction that one of its disjuncts is true, regardless of whether the other disjuncts are true, false, or without truth-value, then (5) seems to generate the paradox. For if (5) is true, every disjunct is false and hence (5) must be false. If (5) is false, its first disjunct is true and hence (5) must be true. If (5) has no truth-value, its second disjunct is true, and hence (5) is true and so has truth-value. Since (5) is conceded to be well-formed, we need not consider the possibility that it is not. None of this is affected by restricting the range of applicability of 'is true' (and 'is false') to those sentences that have a truth-value.

The reasons why so far Martin's apparatus does not serve to neutralize (5) are that (5) is a disjunction he accepts as well-formed and that he also accepts in this paper the rule that a disjunction is true if one of its disjuncts is (whether or not the other disjuncts have a truth-value). But a complication enters because, I believe, both here and in his earlier paper on Grelling's paradox, he also accepts a rule about molecular <u>predicates</u> that is inconsistent with this. And in fact it is his treatment of molecular predicates that finally seems to yield a way out of the Strengthened Liar while preserving the general possibility of self-reference.

Martin's move is to place restrictions on the range of application of molecular predicates. The range of application of a molecular predicate is a function of the ranges of application of its components. He tells us that the range of application of a molecular predicate is the <u>intersection</u> of the ranges of application of its components. Thus in (5) the intersection of the ranges of the disjuncts, as specified by Martin, is the set of true or false sentences. So if we regard (5) as a molecular <u>predicate</u> applied to <u>a</u>, the essential move in the generation of the Strengthened Liar — going from the assumption that the sentence has no truth-value to the conclusion that it must be true — is blocked, because if <u>a</u> has no truth-value then the molecular predicate exemplified in (5) cannot apply to it even if one of its component predicates does.

This restriction on molecular predicates seems to me a high price to pay for getting out of the Strengthened Liar. But as I mentioned, in the present paper Martin presents a system which incorporates the rule that a disjunction is true if one of its disjuncts is (regardless of whether the other disjuncts have truth-value or not). He cannot have that rule and also this proposed restriction on molecular predicates. (5) can be viewed either as a disjunction or as a disjunctive predicate applied to <u>a</u>. Under the assumption that (5) has no truth-value, the restriction on molecular predicates yields a different conclusion about the truth-value of (5) than the one gotten from the rule about disjunctions. From the first rule we cannot move to the conclusion that (5) must therefore be true, but from the second, since it has a true disjunct, we can.

The inconsistency of the two rules, of course, does not show up just in the problem cases, but also in, for example:

(6) The number 3 is red or the number 3 is even.

Thought of as a molecular predicate applied to the number 3, this sentence has no truth-value on Martin's criterion for molecular predicates (presuming, of course, that the range of application of 'is red' and 'is even' do not overlap). But according to the rule for disjunctions, the sentence is true.

I am not altogether sure why Martin does not at this point adopt what seems to me a much more plausible principle, namely, that any molecular sentence with a component that has no truth-value is itself without truth-value. (This would amount to the rules for Bochvar's "internal" connectives discussed by Herzberger.) This would make the local repairs I mentioned earlier. But we are still left with what seems to me a paradox. In order to deal with the Strengthened Liar we posit that some sentences (or propositions, etc.) have no truth-value, while, of course, others are true or false. But then it turns out that we must restrict the range of applicability of the predicates, 'is true' and 'is false', to those sentences that are one or the other. We then cannot say truly of some sentence that has no truth-value that it does not (even though that is exactly what we want to say about a sentence that generates the Strengthened Liar), because to do so would be to say that the sentence is not true and not false. How there can be a set of things with three mutually exclusive subsets about which it is neither true nor false that a member of one of the subsets is not a member of the other two, I find very puzzling — perhaps even more so than the Strengthened Liar itself.

The Range of Truth and Falsity

by Newton Garver

I want to discuss the attacks on the Liar paradox in the light of general considerations about meaning and truth. In particular I want to discuss Martin's attack. Martin is entirely right that the Liar involves questions about the philosophy of language, and that it does so because it has to do with concepts which are critical for understanding and describing language, concepts such as <u>sentence</u>, <u>negation</u>, <u>meaning</u>, and <u>truth</u>. Martin stops the paradox by treating what Epimenides says (or what some sentence says) as a sentence that lacks truth or falsity because it somehow lacks meaning (is semantically incorrect), an attack which requires restricting ourselves to choice-negation (rather than exclusion-negation). Martin is undoubtedly right that what somehow lacks meaning cannot have a truth-value, but even this aspect of his proposal raises some further questions.

It is quite clear that there are varieties of meaning and corresponding varieties of ways in which a sentence, or a string of vocables, can fail to express something true. While there is no definitive way in which to classify varieties of meaning (and meaninglessness), at least five sorts must be considered:

1. grammatical
2. definitional
3. referential
4. categorial
5. situational

The first depends on whether the formal linguistic requirements for a string of vocables being a declarative sentence have been met. These requirements are stated in terms of patterns of stress and pitch, "function words," and gross word-classes such as <u>noun</u>, <u>verb</u>, <u>adjective</u>, etc. If a string of vocables is not grammatically meaningful there are still questions that can be raised about its "meaning" but it is difficult to see how it could fall within the range of applicability (RA) of true or false. The second has to do with whether the general words in the sentence have some established or prescribed meaning. In <u>Jabberwocky</u> Lewis Carroll gives an attractive instance of a grammatically meaningful sentence that falls outside the range of truth and falsity because it contains words that lack definitional meaning:

> 'Twas brillig and the slithy toves
> Did gyre and gimble in the wabe.

The third, referential meaning is characteristic of proper names and other referring expressions. A sentence is unobjectionable (nondeviant) with respect to referential meaning if and only if there actually exist such objects as are signified by its constituent referring expressions. (For the present I make the contestable assumption that referential meaning can be construed as inhering in the language rather than as requiring contextual considerations.) Fiction is a form of storytelling that lies outside the realm of truth and falsity because its proper names are referentially deviant.

There is general agreement that a sentence or statement falls within the RA of true and false only if the criteria of grammatical, definitional, and referential meaning are satisfied: being meaningful in these respects is the minimum condition for a sentence's being a truth-claim. Some have held that these criteria also constitute a sufficient condition for being a truth-claim. Frege's insistence that concepts have sharp boundaries, so that every concept is defined to be either true or false of every object, is an instance of such a view. Tarski's theory of truth might be regarded as another instance, in which gross word-classes are supplemented by specification of logical type or language level so that all self-referential sentences are said to be grammatically (syntactically) deviant. But regarding these three criteria of meaning as a sufficient condition for the RA of true and false involves tampering with one or another of the criteria—with definitional meaning in Frege's case and with grammaticality in Tarski's case. Thus Frege requires us to regard nonsensical sentences as false (the square root of three is purple), and Tarski requires us to regard true statements as nonsensical (this very sentence consists of seven words). Martin is surely right that the first three sorts of meaning do not provide a sufficient condition for the RA of true and false, and his investigation of the fourth sort is much to be welcomed.

The epistemological significance of categories is an ancient and important philosophical topic, dating at least from Plato. In the Sophist Plato asked the question whether all Forms combine with all Forms or whether no Form combines with any other, rejected both hypotheses, and indicated that the real problem is determining which Forms combine with which others. Having raised the problem Plato says little about how to recognize categories or about what detailed categorial restrictions will be required, but others have attempted to fill in the details, including such diverse thinkers as Aristotle, Descartes, Kant, and Ryle. Martin joins their company by proposing that a sentence must satisfy the categorial criterion if it is to fall within the RA of <u>true</u> and <u>false</u>. Thus sentences such as

<u>The</u> <u>square</u> <u>root</u> <u>of</u> <u>three</u> <u>is</u> <u>purple</u>
<u>It</u> <u>is</u> <u>seven</u> o'clock <u>at</u> <u>the</u> <u>South</u> <u>Pole</u>
<u>Colorless</u> <u>green</u> <u>ideas</u> <u>sleep</u> <u>furiously</u>

are, although they satisfy the first three criteria, excluded from the RA of <u>true</u> and <u>false</u> because they fail to satisfy the categorial meaning criterion—although exactly how to describe the categories involved and state the restrictions violated remains to be specified. The Liar paradox is resolved by showing how, without excluding all self-reference, the sentence

<u>This</u> <u>very</u> <u>sentence</u> <u>is</u> <u>false</u>

can be seen to be excluded from the RA of <u>true</u> and <u>false</u> by the categorial criterion.

Aside from the implications of applying his categorial criterion of meaning to the Liar, upon which Donnellan has commented in detail, there are two questions to be raised about Martin's discussion. The first has to do with Martin's characterization of sentences that fail to satisfy the categorial criterion, such as those cited above, as "semantically incorrect." In fact they are not so much incorrect as they are useless from the point of view of epistemology, since they fall outside the RA of <u>true</u> and <u>false</u>. Martin explicitly acknowledges that metaphors often involve deviation from categorial restrictions, and it seems unduly disparaging to label all such metaphors 'semantically incorrect.' The terminology implies rejection, whereas an important task in the philosophy of language is to consider when category restrictions are appropriate and when deviation from them is appropriate. 'Deviant', although not altogether free from negative overtones, seems a better word than 'incorrect', since it makes more sense to investigate when it is proper to deviate from norms than when it is proper to be incorrect.

The second question is whether, as Martin holds, the first four criteria of meaning provide a sufficient condition for the RA of <u>true</u> and <u>false</u>. The alternative is that in order to determine the RA of <u>true</u> and <u>false</u> we must take account of situational factors not involved in the preceding sorts of meaning. It is clear that a sentence that satisfies the first four criteria may be "meaningless" in a context where it is altogether out of place, and also that a given sentence may have to be understood differently in different circumstances. The latter occurs not only when indexical words are involved, such as here, now, you, and I, but also in knowing what sort of speech-act an utterance presents. Consider, for example, the sentence

It is very chilly with that window open.

This sentence is implicitly indexical with respect to time and place, and requires some contextual specification with respect to the word 'that'; therefore different utterances of the sentence may differ in meaning and in truth-value. Such considerations provide one sort of argument for including a situational criterion among those required for specifying the RA of true and false. Let us suppose what is certainly not obvious, that these considerations can be met without admitting a situational criterion—for example, by some modification of what is taken into account as referential meaning. Then we are left with the problem that not all occurrences of the sentence are truth-claims at all. Consider the following situations in which the above sentence might occur: (1) Husband and wife are preparing for guests, one utters the sentence, and the other replies "You're right, but we need some fresh air." (2) A has bragged to B that he can keep his study cool by keeping a certain window open. It is now uncomfortably hot in the study, with the window open; B utters the sentence, and A replies (smiling) "You're right." (3) There is an open window and a draft, and an elderly, rather fragile guest utters the sentence to her young hostess. In the first situation the sentence is used to make a truth-claim, and the response shows clearly enough that what was said falls under the RA of true. In the second situation the sentence is used to make a point ironically, and the same assenting reply does not acknowledge the sentence as true but rather acknowledges the irony as appropriate. In the third situation the sentence is used to make a request, and to respond just by agreeing, disagreeing, or checking the thermometer would be a gross misunderstanding of the import of what the guest said. In the latter two situations the sentence does not fall within the RA of true and false—or at any rate not within the RA of 'is true' or 'is false'. Martin is, of course, aware of indexicals and explicitly takes note of the importance of speech-acts, but he does not appear to appreciate the extent to which these considerations provide the basis for another argument for including a situational meaning criterion among those required for determining the RA of true and false.

These remarks about the five different criteria of meaningfulness are connected quite directly with Donnellan's rather gloomy vision of the prospects for resolving the Liar paradox while restricting our attention to sentences. The question whether the RA of true and false can be specified in terms of the first four sorts of meaning alone is equivalent to the question whether it is really sentences, rather than statements or propositions, that fall under the RA of true and false. A sentence, as Ryle has pointed out, is either a German sentence or a French sentence, but is not said to be made in German or French; whereas a statement (or proposition) is made in German or French but is not thereby a German or French statement. A sentence, that is, is part of language in the abstract; it is a type rather than a token, and whether or not it has meaning as a sentence can be determined by applying the first, second, and fourth criteria. A statement, on the other hand, is part of language-in-use rather than language in the abstract; in de Saussure's terms it belongs to speech (la parole) rather than to language (la langue); it is a sentence-token rather than a sentence, and its meaning as a sentence-token involves not just its sentence meaning but also the contextual meaning of the third and fifth criteria. (At least the meaning of a statement involves the fifth criterion; I want to avoid for purposes of this discussion the interesting and important question of how the third and fifth criteria are related to one another and whether they can be conceived separately.) I believe the prospects for resolving the Liar paradox without having to pay an exorbitant price would be considerably brighter if attention were focused on statements (or propositions, or sentences-in-context) rather than on sentences, as Martin has done; that is, if a contextual meaning criterion were utilized in determining the range of truth and falsity.

Notice that Donnellan has objected to Martin's position because of a counterintuitive relation that would have to exist between the set of sentences and its proper and exclusive subsets. The class of mammals, for instance, has proper and exclusive subclasses, and for any mammal it is possible to say whether or not it belongs to any given subclass. The anomaly with the set of sentences and its putative subsets is that there are, as Donnellan has shown, sentences that belong to one subset and yet which cannot be said not to belong to the other subsets. One simple way to escape from this paradoxical situation is by holding that it is statements rather than sentences that fall within the range of truth and falsity, so that the set of things that are true and the set of things that are false are not subsets of the set of sentences at all.

All of the principal papers in this volume focus their attention on sentences, and amont the contributors, as I have understood the papers presented, only Kearns and Fitch have taken statements or propositions seriously in the sense that they regard statements or propositions (or sentences-in-context) rather than sentences as the sort of things that fall under the RA of true and *false* and as the sort of things that one has to talk about when dealing with the Liar paradox in its various forms. The price tags on the solutions presented in the major papers have been shown to be very high, and I believe the symposium will have helped us all to advance toward a readiness to move forward from the solutions presented here, just as we are all now ready to reject and move forward from Tarski's language levels approach. The more we study semantics the more we become aware of the necessity of looking at wider questions of meaningfulness and meaning criteria. The kind of considerations that have been offered in these papers are certainly wider than those allowed in Tarski's approach; but it seems to me that they are not yet wide enough, and that we have to go beyond the syntactic, the definitional, the categorial, and even the referential criteria of meaning and look instead upon the difference between statements and sentences as relevant to the paradox, a move that will require us to take account of situational criteria of meaning as well.

Reply to Donnellan and Garver

by Robert L. Martin

I

As I understand Donnellan's remarks on my paper, he has presented two objections. One is technical in nature, and the problem can be handled, as he says, by local repairs. I will try to make the repairs, which have to do with the treatment of molecular sentences, but in a way that is different from the way Donnellan suggests. The other objection concerns my restriction of the range of applicability of the predicates 'is true' and 'is false'; this objection is, as he says, more fundamental. I think this objection can be met also, but to do so within the precise framework of the formal language I have presented would seem to require substantial addition and modification. I think I can make clear, informally, a category-approach answer to the question he raises, and that is all I shall attempt at present.

Before turning to the two objections, I would like to note briefly that an impression Donnellan gives is incorrect. He correctly indicates that in the present paper I am primarily concerned with the Strengthened Liar, whereas in my earlier papers on the Liar and Grelling paradoxes I was exclusively concerned, except in the final section of the latter paper, with the ordinary forms of the paradoxes. He is also correct in noting that the strictures against exclusion negation, as well as the restriction on compound predicates, are new moves which are proposed to deal with the Strengthened Liar. But I think there is also the suggestion in what he says that yet another piece of machinery, and this one the heaviest and most unwieldy, is imported to deal with the Strengthened Liar—namely, the restriction of the range of applicability of the predicates 'is true' and 'is false' to the set of sentences that have a truth-value. He writes:

> It turns out, however, that abandoning excluding negation does not suffice, by itself, to block the Strengthened Liar. One must also, as Martin does, restrict the range of applicability of the predicates, "is true" and "is false."[1]

1. K. Donnellan, "Categories, Negation, and the Liar Paradox," this volume, p. 115.

To return to Martin's treatment of the Strengthened Liar, it turns out that since having only one kind of negation, choice-negation, does not suffice to solve the paradox, he must also limit the range of application of the predicates "is true" and "is false," to those sentences that have a truth-value.[2]

Now it may seem something of a quibble, but for the sake of the record I do wish to point out that the restriction of the range of 'is true' and 'is false' to sentences with truth-value is not something tacked onto the category approach to the Liar in an effort to make it work for the Strengthened Liar. Rather it is an essential part of the original approach. It is clear that without this restriction the solution proposed in "Toward a Solution to the Liar Paradox" would not work. To the extent that this restriction is undesirable, the whole category approach to the Liar is undesirable. And on the other hand, in case the category treatment of the Strengthened Liar can be successfully defended, it should not be thought as ad hoc as Donnellan's remarks make it appear.

Local Repairs

I was wrong to say that there is an interpretation for the formalized language I presented under which the open sentence:

$$\sim Tx \text{ v} \sim Vx \text{ v} \sim Sx,$$

with assignments to the predicates as suggested, is satisfied by the mixed set containing exactly the false sentences, the truth-valueless sentences, and the nonsentences. For under such an interpretation the sentence

$$\sim Ta \text{ v} \sim Va \text{ v} \sim Sa$$

(where I(a) = '$\sim Ta \text{ v} \sim Va \text{ v} \sim Sa$') belongs to the set of truth-valueless sentences, but the open sentence is not satisfied by that sentence. That the sentence just mentioned is truth-valueless according to the semantics of the formalized language I devised can be seen from the definition of truth that appears in Appendix B, and especially note 10. My statement on page 99, that a disjunction is true if one of its disjuncts are true, is inconsistent with the definition of truth, as is shown by the case in question (for '$\sim Va$' is true under I, but the disjunction that contains it is without truth-value). I did not realize when writing the paper that my generalization about the truth of disjunctions was incompatible with the formal definition. In first considering how to treat disjunctions to avoid the problem pointed out by Donnellan, I formulated a restriction as an attempt to capture the intuition (such as it is) behind the restriction on compound

2. Ibid., p. 117.

predicates mentioned in "On Grelling's Paradox." But then I dis-
covered, with some embarrassment, that the restriction is actually a consequence of the definition of "true sentence under an interpretation" given in detail in Appendix B. I will first state the
restriction and then provide what rationale I can for it.

A disjunction of one-place atomic sentences with the same term
(individual constant, designator) occurring in each atom is without truth-value if either atom is without truth-value.

What I have in mind is that sentences such as 'Fa v Ga' can be
thought of as the predication of the "predicate," 'Fx v Gx', to the
object denoted by 'a'. In accordance with the restriction on compound predicates, where the RA of the compound predicate is taken
to be no more inclusive than that of whichever component predicate
has the smaller RA, I take the RA of 'Fx v Gx' to be the intersection of RA(F) and RA(G). Hence, where the object denoted by 'a'
does not belong to the RA of, say, 'F', 'Fa v Ga' is without truth-
value, even if 'Ga' is true.

The contrast is with a sentence such as 'Fa v Gb', which can
be thought of as the predication to the individuals that constitute
the ordered pair ⟨a, b⟩ of the two-place "predicate," 'Fx v Gy'.
Here it seems necessary only to require, for the truth of the disjunction, that either 'Fa' or 'Gb' be true. The restriction on compound predicates does not apply since, loosely put, there is no <u>one</u>
thing (an individual or <u>n</u>-tuple of individuals) such that <u>it</u> is being
said to be either F or G.

Donnellan's Second Point

But we are still left with what seems to me a paradox. In
order to deal with the Strengthened Liar we posit that some
sentences (or propositions, etc.) have no truth-value, while,
of course, others are true or false. But then it turns out that
we must restrict the range of applicability of the predicates,
"is true" and "is false," to those sentences that are one or
the other. <u>We then cannot say truly of some sentence that has
no truth-value that it does not</u> (even though that is exactly what
we want to say about a sentence that generates the Strengthened Liar), because to do so would be to say that the sentence
is not true and not false. <u>How there can be a set of things with
three mutually exclusive subsets about which it is neither true
nor false that a member of one of the subsets is not a member
of the other two</u>, I find very puzzling—perhaps even more so
than the Strengthened Liar itself.[3] (emphasis added)

3. Ibid., pp. 122.

There are actually two closely related points, indicated by the underlining. The first I have dealt with elsewhere, and I will review my answer; the second can be handled in much the same way as the first, but necessitates adjustments that I did not anticipate.

On my view, there are sentences without truth-value, and surely one has to be able to say this (I just did). This appears equivalent to saying of such a sentence, S, that it is neither true nor false. But then it appears to follow that S is both not true and not false, and hence that S is not true. And yet this conclusion—that S is not true—is one which, on my view, is itself without truth-value, since the 'not' is to be construed as choice-negation, and the RA of 'is true' is restricted to sentences with truth-value.

In "Toward a Solution to the Liar Paradox," pages 306 and 307, I noted that some disjunctive predicates "span" an entire category and suggested that such predicates be regarded as having the same RA as the "family-name" predicate for that category. In these very special cases it is clear that the parts of the disjunctive predicates function as they do because of their association with the other parts, so it is not unnatural to deny, in these cases, the inference from the semantical correctness of a sentence of the form 'x is P or Q' to the semantical correctness of sentences of the forms 'x is P' and 'x is Q'. In the present case we have a sentence ('S is without truth-value') which we can construe as the negation of a sentence with just such a disjunctive predicate ('It is not the case that S is true or false'). This sentence is true, where S is semantically incorrect, but we cannot break up the parts of the predicate, producing 'S is not true', and expect to have retained semantical correctness.

I should mention that, in the formal language I presented, the counterpart to 'S does not have truth-value' is, under the appropriate interpretation, true, while that of 'S is neither true nor false' is without truth-value. This is technically more convenient but does not reflect the fact that I have relied on above, namely, that often in ordinary speech a disjunctive predicate that spans a category has the force of the corresponding category-predicate. Just where we cut the argument from the truth of 'S is without truth-value' to the truth of 'S is not true' seems not so important, as long as it is cut, and I think I have given some basis for doing so, and indicated the very special circumstances in which an argument of such a form must be barred.

The second point can be put in the form of a two-premise argument. Presumably, I want to accept as true the premises (1) and (2), but must reject as without truth-value the conclusion (3):

    (1) The set of sentences includes three mutually exclusive and exhaustive subsets: the set T of true sentences, the set F of false sentences, and the set R (remainder) of sentences without truth-value.

(2) The Strengthened Liar sentence S belongs to R.
Hence, (3) S does not belong to T.

Since Donnellan would construe (3) as "S is not true" (I assume
this, since the latter is the sentence we have both been considering, which my view forces me to reject), I judge that he would
agree to construe (1) as

(1') For every sentence x, x is true or x is false or x is without truth-value.

(or some such (1') where the language of predication, not of set
membership, is used).

Now the truth of (1') depends on the truth of all its instantia-
tions, where the universal quantifier is dropped and each free occurrence of 'x' in what remains is replaced by the name of a sentence. This raises the question of the range of applicability of the
disjunctive "predicate"

(4) x is true or x is false or x is without truth-value

and of the semantical correctness of a sentence such as

(5) S is true or S is false or S is without truth-value

where S is the Strengthened Liar sentence and so without truth-value.

It seems to me that I have two alternatives here: one is to deny that
(5) is semantically correct, from which it follows that (1') is also
semantically incorrect; the other is to allow, as seems intuitively
plausible, that (5) is semantically correct, in fact, true, and to find
some other way to stop the argument from (1) and (2) to (3).

The first way accords with the restriction on the truth of molecular sentences proposed just above; that is, since the single name
'S' occurs throughout, and at least one disjunct is without truth-
value, the entire disjunction is without truth-value. However the
second way now seems to me correct. Consider the open sentence
or "predicate" (4) again. The first two disjuncts constitute a "predicate" that spans the category covered by the single predicate 'has
truth-value', and of course the predicate 'has truth-value' has a
range of applicability not restricted to sentences with truth-value.
In accordance with the point made in "Toward a Solution to the Liar
Paradox," pages 306 and 307, referred to above, it seems correct
to allow the semantical correctness of (5), by allowing the semantical
correctness, first of all, of the sentence which consists of the first
two disjuncts. And then we have, following the same line as above,
good grounds for denying the inference from the semantical correctness of (5) (and hence of (1)) to the semantical correctness of (3),
where the family-member predicate 'is true' is taken out of the
spanning context and predicated by itself of the semantically incorrect sentence S.

I mentioned above that the formal language I presented does not have provisions for extending the ranges of applicability in cases where component predicates together span a category—indeed it is hard to see how this is possible without bringing into the language the notions of category-predicate and family-member predicate.[4] So, with respect to the formal language presented, I cannot yet provide a satisfactory answer to the question Donnellan has raised.

It may seem to the reader that I have, by allowing the truth of a disjunction such as (5), lost the effect of the restriction on disjunctions proposed in the "local repairs" part of this Reply. To review briefly: I want to say that disjunctions are true as long as they have one true disjunct, except if they involve disjunctive "predicates" of the kind specified above. I am now adding that if a disjunctive "predicate" spans a category, then its range of applicability is the same as that of a category-predicate for that category. The effect of this restriction is to restore truth-value to some disjunctions. The question is, have we thus restored truth-value to the problematic sentence

(6) (6) is false or semantically incorrect or a nonsentence

which inspired (at Donnellan's prodding) the original restriction on disjunctions? The answer is "no", since the predicate 'is false' appears in (6) without its category-mate.

I would like to conclude with an analogy to the Donnellan argument, which I think brings out more clearly the intuitions to which I have been appealing. Thinking of the interrogative as one species of sentence (and putting aside, as Donnellan also does, consideration of propositions, etc.), one might say that the set of sentences divides into three mutually exclusive subsets: the set of sentences for which correct answers are known, the set of sentences for which correct answers are not known, and the remainder. A sentence such as 'The book is on the table' is in the remainder set; does it follow that 'The book is on the table' is not a sentence for which a correct answer is known? We seem to have a true first premise, which divides the set of sentences into three mutually exclusive subsets, and a second true premise which identifies a certain declarative sentence as falling in the third of these subsets; yet there seems to be category confusion involved in denying that the sentence falls in the first subset.

---

4. I have attempted something along these lines in a paper entitled "Negation and Semantic Categories" presented at the meeting of the American Philosophical Association, Western Division, May 1969.

II

The first of Garver's questions is whether 'semantically deviant' is not better terminology than 'semantically incorrect'.[5] I think it is indeed better terminology, and for the reasons he gives.

His second question is, as I understand it, whether situational factors should not be included in determining whether a given sentence falls within the RA of the predicates 'is true' and 'is false'. ("The second question is whether, as Martin holds, the first four criteria of meaning provide a sufficient condition for the RA of true and false.")[6] The first four criteria of meaning, we recall, are:

1. grammatical
2. definitional
3. referential
4. categorial

Again I would answer positively, agreeing that there are circumstances in which sentences that are normally true or false are in fact without truth-value. I hesitate to agree that I have held a contrary position, and I suspect it is just my lack of attention to situational considerations that led Garver to suppose that I regard them as irrelevant to the determination of the applicability of 'is true' and 'is false'. I have disregarded these matters, and the theory of speech-acts generally, because I have not seen that they are directly germane to the questions raised by the Liar (I will say more about this later). In fact I have never set out to list conditions sufficient for saying that an entity x falls within the RA of 'is true' or 'is false'; I have been concerned only with arguing that category-correctness (nondeviance) is a necessary condition.

Garver urges that we turn our attention to statements or propositions or sentences-in-contexts, rather than to sentences. One of his arguments concerns Donnellan's criticism (of my position), which involves the subsets of the set of sentences; Garver's point is that I could escape the force of that argument by holding that statements, rather than sentences, fall within the RA of 'is true' and 'is false'. I don't think the move would help, because Donnellan could reformulate his argument as follows (understanding a statement to be, sometimes, the utterance of a sentence in a certain context): The set of utterances of sentences contains three mutually exclusive subsets—those that are true, those that are false, and the remainder. An utterance of a sentence may be a

5. N. Garver, "The Range of Truth and Falsity," this volume, p. 125.
6. Idem.

member of the third set—say it is not an utterance of the right sentence in the right circumstances to constitute the making of a statement—and yet, on Martin's view, it cannot be said not to belong to the first set. I have already tried to answer Donnellan's argument, and I don't think that the switch to statements changes the real force of either his criticism or my reply.

Garver's main point, however, is that the switch from sentences to statements should enable us to find solutions to the Liar with lower price tags than those offered in the major papers of this volume. Perhaps he is right, and it will be interesting to see whether recent developments in the theory of speech-acts and formal pragmatics suggest new approaches to the Liar. The problem, as I see it, is the following. We know (by <u>reductio</u>) that there is no statement which says of itself that it is not true (I am assuming that all statements are true or false, but not both, and that a statement is true if and only if what it says is the case). That is, there is <u>no</u> sentence that <u>ever</u> can be used, in <u>any</u> circumstance, to make such a statement. However, the following <u>appears</u> to be a sentence that could be used in some circumstances to make just such a statement.

(S) The statement which I am now making is not true.

Let us suppose that the situational features are propitious—the speaker is apparently serious and in a statement-making frame of mind. The question is, what is there about the <u>sentence</u> S that keeps it from being used in the manner in which a sentence such as

(R) The statement which I just made is not true

may be used, unproblematically, to make exactly the statement that the speaker seems to be making? Notice that the problem again concerns a <u>sentence</u>—its unfittingness for use in making the statement we <u>expect</u> of it—and that the considerations advanced toward the solution of the sentence-versions of the Liar are immediately relevant.

Ancient and medieval sources are not included. For such references, see The Development of Logic, by William and Martha Kneale (Oxford, 1962), and A History of Formal Logic, by I. M. Bochenski, translated and edited by Ivo Thomas (Notre Dame, Indiana, 1961).

Agassi, J. Variations on the liar's paradox. Studia Logica 15 (1964): 237–38.

Anderson, A. R. Review of Thomson's "On some paradoxes" (Analytic Philosophy, R. J. Butler, ed., Oxford, 1962, pp. 104–19). Journal of Symbolic Logic 29 (1964): 139–40.

Anonymous. Logical paradoxes, puzzles, and problems. Delaware Valley Announcer 35 (1962): 30–31.

Bar-Hillel, Y. The present state of the problem of the antinomies: the semantical antinomies. Tarbits 12 (1940–41): 275–86.

_____. Discussion—the revival of "The liar." Philosophy and Phenomenological Research 8 (1947): 245–53.

_____. New light on the liar. Analysis 18 (1957): 1–6.

_____. Do natural languages contain paradoxes? Studium Generale 19 (1966): 391–97.

_____. More on sentences, statements, the cogito, and the liar. Philosophical Studies 19 (1968): 55–57.

Bausch, A. Review of Pap's "The linguistic hierarchy and the vicious-circle principle" (Philosophical Studies 5 (1954): 49–53). Journal of Symbolic Logic 22 (1957): 392–93.

Baylis, C. Review of Gregory's "Heterological and homological" (Mind 61 (1952): 85–88). Journal of Symbolic Logic 17 (1952): 220.

Beard, Robert W. Semantic theory and the paradox of the non-communicator. Philosophical Studies 17 (1966): 44–45.

Behmann, H. The paradoxes of logic. Mind 46 (1937): 218–21.

Benda, J. Un trouble-fête: l'esprit de rigueur. Revue de métaphysique et de morale 54 (1949): 163–69.

Bennet, J. Review of Mackie's "Self-refutation—a formal analysis" (Philosophical Quarterly 14 (1964): 193–203). Journal of Symbolic Logic 30 (1965): 365–66.

──────. Reviews of the following appeared in the Journal of Symbolic Logic 32 (1967): 108–12:
Encarnacion's "On Ushenko's version of the liar paradox" (Mind 64 (1955): 99–100).
Ushenko's "A note on the liar paradox" (Mind 64 (1955): 543).
Toms's "The liar paradox" (Philosophical Review 65 (1956): 542–47).
Donnellan's "A note on the liar paradox" (Philosphical Review 66 (1957): 394–97).
Ushenko's "An addendum to the note on the liar paradox" (Mind 66 (1957): 98).
Toms's "Reply to a note on the liar paradox" (Philosophical Review 67 (1958): 101–05).
Rozeboom's "Is Epimenides still lying?" (Analysis 18 (1957–58): 105–13).
Huggett's "Paradox lost" (Analysis 19 (1958): 21–23).
Whitely's "Let Epimenides lie!" (Analysis 19 (1958): 23–24).
Sibajiban's "Mr. Eric Toms on the liar paradox" (Mind 74 (1965): 421–23).

Beth, E. W. Some remarks on Dr. Perelman's essay on logical antinomies. Mind 45 (1936): 487–88.

──────. De Paradoxen. Algerneen Nederlands tijdschrift voor wijsbegeerte en psychologie 32 (1938–39): 193–208.

──────. L'état actuel du problème logique des antinomies. Congrès International de Philosophie des Sciences, Paris, 1949. 11 Logique, Actualités scientifiques et industrielles 1134, Paris, Hermann, 1951, pp. 7–14.

Black, M. Review of A. Koyré's Epiménide le menteur (Actualités scientifiques et industrielles 1021, Paris, Hermann, 1947). Journal of Symbolic Logic 13 (1943): 146.

──────. Review of Stegmüller's Das Wahrheitsproblem und die Idee der Semantik (Vienna, 1957). Philosophical Review 67 (1958): 575–77.

Bochenski, I. M. Formalization of a scholastic solution of the paradox of the liar, in Logico-Philosophical Studies, ed. A. Menne (Holland, 1962).

Borel, E. Les Paradoxes de l'infini. L'avenir de la science, no. 25, Paris, 1946, Pt. 3 on Richard's paradox.

Bowden, L. Heterologicality. Analysis 12 (1952): 77–81.

Bradley, C. K. The paradoxes. Astounding Science Fiction 53 (1954): 93–100.

Bröcker, W. Antinomien und Paradoxien in der Logik. Blätter für deutsche Philosophie 12 (1938–39): 365–68.

Brown, D. B. Paradox without tiers. Analysis 17 (1957): 112-18.
Brown, H. C. The logic of Mr. Russell. Journal of Philosophy 8 (1911): 85-91.
Cargile, J. Reviews of the following appeared in the Journal of Symbolic Logic 32 (1967): 408-09:
Geach's "Ryle on namely riders" (Analysis 21 (1961): 64-67).
Fitzpatrick's "'Heterological' and namely-riders" (Analysis 22 (1961): 18-22).
Geach's "Namely riders again" (Analysis 22 (1962): 92-94).
_____. Reviews of the following appeared in the Journal of Symbolic Logic 34 (1969): 645:
Bar-Hillel's "New light on the liar" (Analysis 18 (1957): 1-6).
Bar-Hillel's "Do natural languages contain paradoxes?" (Studium Generale 19 (1966): 391-97).
Carnap, R. Die Antinomien und die Unvollständigkeit der Mathematik. Monats. Math. Phys. 41 (1934): 263-84.
Carruccio, E. On the contradictoriness, according to Dingler, of non-predicative definitions. Methodos 2 (1950-51): 295-96. (In reply to H. Dingler's On the division between subject and object. Methodos 2 (1950): 14-21.)
Church, A. The Richard paradox. The American Mathematical Monthly 41 (1934): 356-61.
_____. Review of Weinberg's "A possible solution of the heterological paradox" (Philosophical Review 46 (1937): 657-59). Journal of Symbolic Logic 3 (1938): 46.
_____. Review of Beth's "De Paradoxen" (Algerneen Nederlands tijdschrift voor wijsbegeerte en psychologie 32 (1938-39): 193-208). Journal of Symbolic Logic 4 (1939): 125.
_____. Review of A. Koyré's "The liar" (Philosophy and Phenomenological Research 6 (1946): 344-62). Journal of Symbolic Logic 11(1946): 131.
_____. Review of Finsler's "Gibt es unentscheidbare Sätze?" (Commentarii Mathematici Helvetici 16 (1944): 310-20). Journal of Symbolic Logic 11 (1946): 131-32.
_____. Review of Geach's "Mr. Ill-named" (Analysis 9 (1948): 14-16). Journal of Symbolic Logic 14 (1949): 136.
_____. Review of Lawrence's "Heterology and hierarchy" (Analysis 10 (1950): 73-76). Journal of Symbolic Logic 15 (1950): 216-17.
_____. Review of Levi's "A propósito de la Nota del Dr. Pi Calleja, Sobre paradojas lógicas y principio del tertium non datur" (Mathematicae Notae 9 (1949): 143-51). Journal of Symbolic Logic 17 (1952): 200-07.
_____. Review of Bradley's "The paradoxes" (Astounding Science Fiction 53 (1954): 93-100). Journal of Symbolic Logic 19 (1954): 236.

_____. Review of Geach's "On insolubilia" (Analysis 15 (1955): 71–72). Journal of Symbolic Logic 20 (1955): 192.

_____. Review of Moch's "On peut éviter les antinomies classiques sans restreindre la notion d'ensemble" (Comptes rendus hebdomadaires des séances de l'Académie des Sciences 242 (1956): 1402–04). Journal of Symbolic Logic 21 (1956): 322.

_____. Review of Mokre's "Zu den logischen Paradoxien" (Meinung-Gedenkschrift, Schriften der Universität Graz 1, "Styria" Steirische Verlagsanstalt, Graz (1952): 81–89). Journal of Symbolic Logic 28 (1963): 106.

Cohen, L. J. Can the logic of indirect discourse be formalized? Journal of Symbolic Logic 22 (1957): 225–32.

_____. Professor Goodstein's formalisation of the policeman. Journal of Symbolic Logic 23 (1958): 420.

_____. Why do Cretans have to say so much? Philosophical Studies 12 (1961): 72–78.

_____. Indirect speech: a rejoinder to Professor A. N. Prior. Philosophical Studies 14 (1963): 15–18.

_____. Indirect speech: a further rejoinder to Professor Prior. Philosophical Studies 15 (1964): 38–40.

Conte, A. G. Review of Rivetti Barbò's L'antinomia del mentitore nel pensiero contemporaneo, da Pierce a Tarski (Milano, 1961). Journal of Symbolic Logic 31 (1966): 283–84.

Curry, B. The paradox of Kleene and Rosser. Transactions of the American Mathematical Society 50 (1941): 454–516.

de Laguna, T. On certain logical paradoxes. Philosophical Review 25 (1916): 16–27.

Dingler, H. On definitions that contain themselves as determinants. Methodos 2 (1950–51): 296–98.

Donnellan, K. S. A note on the liar paradox. Philosophical Review 66 (1957): 394–97.

Drange, T. The paradox of the non-communicator. Philosophical Studies 15 (1964): 92–96.

_____. The paradox defended. Philosophical Studies 18 (1967): 1–12.

Dunn, M. J. Drange's paradox lost. Philosophical Studies 18 (1967): 94–95.

Encarnacion, J. On Ushenko's version of the liar paradox. Mind 64 (1955): 99–100.

Evans, E. On some semantic illusions. Mind 63 (1954): 203–18.

Findlay, J. Gödelian sentences: a non-numerical approach. Mind 51 (1942): 259–65.

Finsler, P. Gibt es unentscheidbare Sätze? Commentarii Mathematici Helvetici 16 (1944): 310–20.

Fitch, F. B. Note on Hofstadter's "On semantic problems." Journal of Philosophy 35 (1938): 360–61.

_____. Review of Tarski's "The semantic conception of truth and the foundations of semantics" (Philosophy and Phenomenological Research 4 (1944): 341-76). Journal of Symbolic Logic 9 (1944): 68.

_____. Review of Ushenko's "A note on the semantic conception of truth" (Philosophy and Phenomenological Research 5 (1944): 104-07). Journal of Symbolic Logic 10 (1945): 22.

_____. Self-reference in philosophy. Mind 55 (1946): 64-73. A revised version appears as Appendix C of Fitch's Symbolic Logic (New York, 1952), pp. 217-25.

_____. Self-referential relations. Actes du Xième congrès international de philosophie 14 (Amsterdam, 1953): 121-27.

_____. Universal metalanguages for philosophy. Review of Metaphysics 17 (1964): 396-402.

Fitzpatrick, P. J. 'Heterological' and namely-riders. Analysis 22 (1961): 18-22.

Geach, P. T. Mr. Ill-named. Analysis 9 (1948): 14-16.

_____. A note on the reflexive paradoxes. Philosophical Review 62 (1953): 427-28.

_____. On insolubilia. Analysis 15 (1955): 71-72.

_____. Ryle on namely-riders. Analysis 21 (1961): 64-67.

_____. Namely-riders again. Analysis 22 (1962): 92-94.

Goddard, L. True and provable. Mind 67 (1958): 13-31.

_____. Sense and nonsense. Mind 73 (1964): 309-31.

Good, I. J. A note on Richard's paradox. Mind 75 (1966): 431.

Goodstein, R. L. On the formalisation of indirect discourse. Journal of Symbolic Logic 23 (1958): 417-19.

Gregory, J. Heterological and homological. Mind 61 (1952): 85-88.

Grelling, K. The logical paradoxes. Mind 45 (1936): 481-86.

_____. Der Einfluss der Antinomien auf die Entwicklung der Logik im 20. Jahrhundert. Travaux du IXième congrès international de philosophie, fasc. VI (1937): 8-17.

Grelling, K., and Nelson, L. Bemerkungen dem Paradoxien von Russell und Burali-Forti. Abhandlungen der Frieschen Schule 2 (1907-08): 300-34.

Guthrie, E. Russell's theory of types. Journal of Philosophy 12 (1915): 381-85.

Harris, R. The semantics of self-description. Analysis 27 (1967): 144.

_____. Self-description and the theory of types. Analysis 28 (1968): 207-08.

Helmer, O. Remarques sur le problème des antinomies. Philosophisches Jahrbuch der Görresgesellschaft 47 (1934): 421-24.

_____. Perelman versus Gödel. Mind 46 (1937): 58-60.

Henle, P. Review of Reach's "The name relation and the logical antinomies" (Journal of Symbolic Logic 3 (1938): 97-111). Journal of Symbolic Logic 4 (1939): 134.

Herzberger, H. G. Paradoxes of grounding in semantics. Journal of Philosophy 67 (1970): 145–67.

Hintikka, J. Identity, variables, and impredicative definitions. Journal of Symbolic Logic 21 (1956): 225–45.

——. Vicious circle principle and the paradoxes. Journal of Symbolic Logic 22 (1957): 245–49.

Hofstadter, A. On semantic problems. Journal of Philosophy 35 (1938): 225–32.

Huggett, W. J. Paradox lost. Analysis 19 (1958): 21–23.

Issmann, S. Le paradoxe du menteur dans les languages naturelles. Logique et analyse 2 (1960): 11–14.

Jensen, R. Review of Hintikka's "Identity, variables, and impredicative definitions" (Journal of Symbolic Logic 21 (1956): 225–45). Journal of Symbolic Logic 32 (1967): 258–59.

——. Review of Hintikka's "Vicious circle principle and the paradoxes" (Journal of Symbolic Logic 22 (1957): 245–49). Journal of Symbolic Logic 32 (1967): 258–59.

Jörgensen, J. Some reflections on reflexivity. Mind 62 (1953): 289–300.

——. On Kattsoff's reflexions on Jörgensen's reflexions on reflexivity. Mind 64 (1955): 542.

Kalmar, L Review of Curry's "The paradox of Kleene and Rosser" (Transactions of the American Mathematical Society 50 (1941): 454–516). Journal of Symbolic Logic 11 (1946): 136–37.

Kanger, S. Reviews of the following appeared in the Journal of Symbolic Logic 32 (1967): 549–50:
  Cohen's "Can the logic of indirect discourse be formalised?" (Journal of Symbolic Logic 22 (1957): 225–32).
  Prior's "Epimenides the Cretan" (Journal of Symbolic Logic 23 (1958): 261–66).
  Goodstein's "On the formalisation of indirect discourse" (Journal of Symbolic Logic 23 (1958): 417–19).
  Cohen's "Professor Goodstein's formalisation of the policeman" (Journal of Symbolic Logic 23 (1958): 420.
  Cohen's "Why do Cretans have to say so much?" (Philosophical Studies 12 (1961): 72–78).
  Prior's "Indirect speech again" (Philosophical Studies 14 (1963): 12–15).
  Cohen's "Indirect speech: a rejoinder to Professor A. N. Prior" (Philosophical Studies 14 (1963): 15–18).
  Prior's "Indirect speech and extensionality" (Philosophical Studies 15 (1964): 35–38).
  Cohen's "Indirect speech: a further rejoinder to Professor Prior" (Philosophical Studies 15 (1964): 38–40).

Kattsoff, L. O. Some reflections on reflexivity. Mind 64 (1955): 96–98.

Kemeny, J. G. Review of Stenius's "Das Problem der logischen Antinomien" (Societas Scientarium Fennica, Commentationes Physico-Mathematicae 14 (1949). Journal of Symbolic Logic 15 (1950): 226–27.

Killalea, J. N. Primeness and heterologicality. Analysis 14 (1953): 20–24.

Kleene, S., and Rosser, J. The inconsistency of certain formal logics. Annals of Mathematics 36 (1935): 630–36.

Kohl, H. R., and Parsons, L. Self-reference, truth, and provability. Mind 69 (1960): 69–73.

Koj, L. Zasada przezroczystośei a antynomie semantyczne. Studia Logica 14 (1963): 227–54.

Koyré, A. The liar. Philosophy and Phenomenological Research 6 (1946): 344–62.

_____. Reply. Philosophy and Phenomenological Research 8 (1947): 254–55.

_____. Epiménide le menteur (Ensemble et Categorie). Actualités scientifiques et industrielles 1021, Paris, Hermann, 1947.

Kutschera, F. Die Antinomien der Logik: semantische Untersuchungen (Freiburg, 1964).

Lambert, K. On the non-communicator. Philosophical Studies 17 (1966): 27–30.

Landsberg, P. On heterological paradoxes. Mind 62 (1953): 379–81.

Langford, C. H. Review of C. H. Perelman's "Les paradoxes de la logique" (Mind 45 (1936): 204–08). Journal of Symbolic Logic 1 (1936): 65–66.

_____. Review of Grelling's "The logical paradoxes" (Mind 45 (1936): 481–86). Journal of Symbolic Logic 2 (1937): 60.

_____. Review of Beth's "Some remarks on Dr. Perelman's essay on logical antinomies" (Mind 45 (1936): 487–88). Journal of Symbolic Logic 2 (1937): 60.

_____. Review of Behmann's "The paradoxes of logic" (Mind 46 (1937): 218–21). Journal of Symbolic Logic 2 (1937): 92.

_____. Review of Ushenko's "A new Epimenides" (Mind 46 (1937): 549–50). Journal of Symbolic Logic 3 (1938): 51.

_____. Review of MacIver's "More about some old logical puzzles" (Analysis 6 (1938): 63–68). Journal of Symbolic Logic 6 (1941): 104.

_____. On paradoxes of the type of the Epimenides. Mind 56 (1947): 350.

_____. The paradoxes. Journal of Philosophy 47 (1950): 777–78.

Langford, C. H., and Langford, M. The logical paradoxes. Philosophy and Phenomenological Research 21 (1959): 110–13.

Lawrence, N. Heterology and hierarchy. Analysis 10 (1950): 73–76. Reprinted in M. MacDonald, ed., Philosophy and Analysis (Oxford, New York, 1954).

Levi, B. A propósito de la nota del Dr. Pi Calleja. Sobre paradojas logicas y principio del tertium non datur. Mathematicae Notae 9 (1949): 143–51.

Lévy, P. Les paradoxes de la théorie des ensembles infinis. Recherches philosophiques 6 (1936–37): 204–19.

_____. Review of Borel's "Les paradoxes de l'infini (L'avenir de la science, no. 25, Paris, 1946). Bulletin des Sciences Mathematiques 73 (1949): 180–86.

Lindley, T. F. 'True' and 'false'. Journal of Philosophy 61 (1964): 387–95.

Lipps, H. Bemerkungen zu der Paradoxie des Lügners. Kant-Studien 28 (1923): 335–39.

Lorenzen, P. Review of Beth's "L'état actuel du problème logique des antinomies" (Congrès international de philosophie des sciences, Paris, 1949. 11 Logique, Actualités scientifiques et industrielles 1134, Paris, Hermann, 1951, pp. 7–14). Journal of Symbolic Logic 22 (1957): 369.

Lupasco, S. Review of Borel's "Les Paradoxes de l'infini (L'avenir de la science, no. 25, Paris, 1946). Revue Philosophique de la France et de l'Etranger 139 (1949): 93–95.

MacIver, A. M. More about some old logical puzzles. Analysis 6 (1938): 63–68.

Mackie, J. S., and Smart, J. J. C. A variant of the 'heterological' paradox. Analysis 13 (1953): 61–65.

_____. A variant of the 'heterological' paradox—a further note. Analysis 14 (1954): 146–49.

McKinsey, J. C. C. Review of Ushenko's "Undecidable statements and metalanguage" (Mind 53 (1944): 258–62). Journal of Symbolic Logic 9 (1944): 97–98.

McNaughton, R. Review of Wang's "The irreducibility of impredicative principles" (Mathematische Annalen 125 (1952): 56–66). Journal of Symbolic Logic 18 (1953): 265–66.

Martin, R. L. Toward a solution to the liar paradox. Philosophical Review 76 (1967): 279–311.

_____. On Grelling's paradox. Philosophical Review 7 (1968): 321–31.

_____. Sommers on denial and negation. Nous 3 (1969): 219–26.

Martin, R. M. Review of Stegmüller's Das Wahrheitsproblem und die Idee der Semantik (Vienna, 1957). Journal of Symbolic Logic 31 (1966): 496.

Matheson, G. Concerning 'sense and nonsense'. Mind 78 (1969): 116–20.

Meager, R. Heterologicality and the liar. Analysis 16 (1956): 131–38.

Menger, K. The new logic (trans. by H. B. Gottlieb and J. K. Senior). Philosophy of Science 4 (1937): 299–336.

Moch, F. On peut éviter les antinomies classiques sans restreindre la notion d'ensemble. Comptes rendus hebdomadaires des séances de l'Académie des Sciences 242 (1956): 1402–04.

Mokre, J. Zu den logischen Paradoxien. Meinung-Gedenkschrift, Schriften der Universität Graz 1, "Styria" Steirische Verlagsanstalt, Graz (1952): 81–89.

Mostowski, A. Review of Fitch's "Self-reference in philosophy" (Mind 55 (1946): 64–73). Journal of Symbolic Logic 11 (1946): 95–96.

_____. Some impredicative definitions in the axiomatic set-theory. Fundamenta Mathematicae 37 (1950–51): 111–24.

_____. Correction to the paper "Some impredicative definitions in the axiomatic set-theory." Fundamenta Mathematicae 38 (1951–52): 238.

Müller, G. H. Review of Yuting's "Two semantical paradoxes" (Journal of Symbolic Logic 20 (1955): 119–20). Journal of Symbolic Logic 21 (1956): 380.

Myhill, J. A system which can define its own truth. Fundamenta Mathematicae 37 (1950): 190–92.

Nagel, E. Review of Hofstadter's "On semantic problems" (Journal of Philosophy 35 (1938): 225–32). Journal of Symbolic Logic 3 (1938): 90.

_____. Review of Northrop's Riddles in Mathematics: A Book of Paradoxes (New York, 1944). Journal of Symbolic Logic 10 (1945): 21.

Nell, E. No proposition can describe itself. Analysis 26 (1966): 147–48.

_____. Semantics and self-description. Analysis 28 (1967): 32.

Nelson, E. Review of Ushenko's The Problems of Logic (London, Princeton, 1941). Journal of Symbolic Logic 6 (1941): 166–68.

Northrop, E. P. Riddles in Mathematics: A Book of Paradoxes (New York, 1944).

O'Carroll, M. J. Improper self-reference in classical logic and the prediction paradox. Logique et analyse 10 (1967): 167–72.

_____. A three-valued, non-levelled logic consistent for all self-reference. Logique et analyse 10 (1967): 173–78.

O'Connor, J. On eliminating self-reference. Analysis 28 (1968): 131–32.

Orey, S. Reviews of the following appeared in the Journal of Symbolic Logic 20 (1955): 291–93:

  Bowden's "Heterologicality" (Analysis 12 (1952): 77–81).

Landsberg's "On heterological paradoxes" (Mind 62 (1953): 379-81).

Mackie and Smart's "A variant of the 'heterological' paradox" (Analysis 13 (1953): 61-65).

Killalea's "Primeness and heterologicality" (Analysis 14 (1953): 20-24).

Mackie and Smart's "A variant of the 'heterological' paradox— a further note" (Analysis 14 (1954): 146-49).

Lawrence's "Heterology and hierarchy" (as it appears in M. Macdonald, ed., Philosophy and Analysis (Oxford, New York, 1954).

Ryle's "Heterologicality" (as it appears in M. MacDonald, ed. Philosophy and Analysis (Oxford, New York, 1954).

Pap, A. The linguistic hierarchy and the vicious-circle principle. Philosophical Studies 5 (1954): 49-53.

Perelman, C. H. Les paradoxes de la logique. Mind 45 (1936): 204-08.

_____. Réponse à MM. Grelling et Beth. Mind 46 (1937): 278-79.

_____. Review of Koyré's Epiménide le menteur. Revue philosophique de la France et de l'Etranger 139 (1949): 235-38.

Popper, K. Self-reference and meaning in ordinary language. Mind 63 (1954): 162-69. Reprinted in Conjectures and Refutations: The Growth of Scientific Knowledge (London, 1963): 304-11.

Prior, A. N. Epimenides the Cretan. Journal of Symbolic Logic 23 (1958): 261-66.

_____. Review of Fitch's "Self-referential relations" (Actes du Xième Congrès international de philosophie 14 (Amsterdam, 1953): 121-27). Journal of Symbolic Logic 24 (1959): 240.

_____. On a family of paradoxes. Notre Dame Journal of Formal Logic 2 (1961): 16-32.

_____. Indirect speech again. Philosophical Studies 14 (1963): 12-15.

_____. Indirect speech and extensionality. Philosophical Studies 15 (1964): 35-38.

Quine, W. V. Review of Saarino's "Zur heterologischen Paradoxie" (Theoria 3 (1937): 38-56). Journal of Symbolic Logic 2 (1937): 138.

_____. Review of Grelling's "Der Einfluss der Antinomien auf die Entwicklung der Logik im 20. Jahrhundert (Travaux du IXième Congrès international de philosophie, fasc. VI (1937): 8-17). Journal of Symbolic Logic 2 (1937): 174.

_____. Review of Menger's "The new logic" (trans. by H. B. Gottlieb and J. K. Senior) (Philosophy of Science 4 (1937): 299-336). Journal of Symbolic Logic 3 (1938): 48.

_____. Review of Lévy's "Les paradoxes de la théorie des ensembles infinis" (Recherches Philosophiques 6 (1936-37): 204-19). Journal of Symbolic Logic 4 (1938): 102.

_____. Review of Bröcker's "Antinomien und Paradoxien in der Logik" (Blätter für deutsche Philosophie 12 (1938-39): 365-68). Journal of Symbolic Logic 5 (1940): 79.

_____. Review of Saarino's "Der Begriff der Hierarchie und die Logischen Paradoxien" (Proceedings of the Tenth International Congress of Philosophy (Amsterdam, 1949): 785-90). Journal of Symbolic Logic 14 (1949): 131.

_____. Paradox. Scientific American 206 (1962): 84-86. Reprinted in The Ways of Paradox and Other Essays (New York, 1966).

Quiney, H. R. A non-hierarchical mathematical logic. Australasian Journal of Philosophy 10 (1932): 216-21.

Reach, K. The name relation and the logical antinomies. Journal of Symbolic Logic 3 (1938): 97-111.

_____. The name relation and the logical antinomies. Erkenntnis 7 (1938): 236-40. (A summary of the above.)

Rescher, N. Discussion—semantic paradoxes and the propositional analysis of indirect discourse. Philosophy of Science 28 (1961): 437-40.

_____. A note on self-referential statements. Notre Dame Journal of Formal Logic 5 (1964): 218-20.

Resnik, M. D. Professor Goddard and the simple theory of types. Mind 77 (1968): 565-68.

Richards, T. J. Self-referential paradoxes. Mind 76 (1967): 387-403.

Richman, R. J. On the self-reference of a meaning theory. Philosophical Studies 4 (1953): 69-72.

Riverso, E. Il Paradosso del mentitore. Rassegna di Scienze Filosofiche 13 (1960): 296-325.

Rivetti Barbò, F. Le antinomie concettuali ed il paradosso di Russell. Rivista di Filosofia neo-scolastica 49 (1957): 146-80.

_____. Formalismo, paradossi e logica. Rivista di Filosofia neo-scolastica 50 (1958): 305-25.

_____. L'origine dei paradossi ed il regresso all'infinito. Rivista di Filosofia neo-scolastica 51 (1959): 27-60.

_____. Natura dei sistemi formali e genesi dei paradossi. Atti del XII Congresso Internazionale di Filosofia 4 (1960): 287-93.

_____. L'antinomia del mentitore nel pensiero contemporaneo, da Pierce a Tarski, Studi—testi—bibliografia (Milano, 1961).

Rogers, R. A survey of formal semantics. Synthese 15 (1963): 17-56 (esp. pp. 18-19).

Ross, A. On self-reference and a puzzle in constitutional law. Mind 78 (1969): 1-24.

Rozeboom, W. W. Is Epimenides still lying? Analysis 18 (1957–58): 105–13.

Russell, B. Les paradoxes de la logique. Revue de métaphysique et de morale 14 (1906): 627–50.

_____. Mathematical logic as based on the theory of types. American Journal of Mathematics 30 (1908): 222–62.

Rüstow, A. Der Lügner, Theorie, Geschichte und Auflösung, dissertation. Erlangen, Teubner Verl. (Leipzig, 1910).

Ryle, G. Heterologicality. Analysis 11 (1951): 61–69. Reprinted in M. MacDonald, ed., Philosophy and Analysis (Oxford, New York, 1954).

Saarino, U. Zur heterologischen Paradoxie. Theoria 3 (1937): 38–56.

_____. Der Begriff der Hierarchie und die logischen Paradoxien. Proceedings of the Tenth International Congress of Philosophy (Amsterdam, 1949): 785–90.

Schlesinger, G. Elimination of self-reference. Analysis 27 (1967): 206–08.

Schmidt, P. F. Self-referential justification. Philosophical Studies 8 (1957): 49–54.

Segelberg, I. Bemerkungen zu einigen logischen Paradoxien. Theoria 9 (1943): 157–62.

Shoenfield, J. R. Review of Smullyan's "Languages in which self-reference is possible" (Journal of Symbolic Logic 22 (1957). Journal of Symbolic Logic 24 (1959): 228.

Sibajiban. Mr. Eric Toms on the liar paradox. Mind 74 (1965): 421–23.

Skinner, R. C. The paradox of the liar. Mind 68 (1959): 322–35.

Skolem, Th. De logiske paradokser og botemidlene mot dem. Norsk Matematisk tidskrift 32 (1950): 2–11.

_____. Review of Mostowski's "Some impredicative definitions in the axiomatic set-theory" (Fundamenta Mathematicae 37 (1950–51): 111–24) Journal of Symbolic Logic 16 (1951): 274–75.

_____. Review of Mos⸱owski's "Correction to the paper 'Some impredicative definitions in the axiomatic set-theory'" (Fundamenta Mathematicae 38 (1951–52): 238). Journal of Symbolic Logic 18 (1953): 343.

Skyrms, B. Return of the liar: three-valued logic and the concept of truth. American Philosophical Quarterly 7 (1970): 153–61.

Smith, H. B. The theory of multiple implication and its application to the generalized problem of Epimenides. Bulletin of The American Mathematical Society 35 (1929): 60–66.

Smullyan, R. M. Languages in which self-reference is possible. Journal of Symbolic Logic 22 (1957): 56–67.

Sommers, F. Predicability in Philosophy in America, Max Black, ed. (Ithaca, 1964).

_____. On concepts of truth in natural languages. Review of Metaphysics 23 (1969): 259–86.

Stegmüller, W. Das Wahrheitsproblem und die Idee der Semantik: Eine Einführung in die Theorien von A. Tarski und R. Carnap (Vienna, 1957).

Stenius, E. Das Problem der logischen Antinomien. Societas Scientarium Fennica, Commentationes Physico-Mathematicae 14 (1949).

Strawson, P. F. Paradoxes, posits, and propositions. Philosophical Review 76 (1967): 214–19.

Stroll, A. Is everyday language inconsistent? Mind 63 (1954): 219–25.

Tarski, A. The concept of truth in formalized languages in Logic, Semantics, Metamathematics: Papers from 1923–38, J. H. Woodger, trans. (Oxford, 1956), pp. 152–278.

_____. The semantic conception of truth and the foundations of semantics. Philosophy and Phenomenological Research 4 (1944): 341–76. Reprinted in Readings in Philosophical Analysis, Feigl and Sellars, eds. (New York, 1949), and in Semantics and the Philosophy of Language, Linsky, ed. (Urbana, 1952).

_____. Truth and proof. Scientific American 220 (1969): 63–77.

Thomas, I. The written liar and Thomas Oliver. Notre Dame Journal of Formal Logic 6 (1965): 201–08.

Thompson, M. H., Jr. The logical paradoxes and Pierce's Semiotic. Journal of Philosophy 46 (1949): 513–36.

Thomson, J. F. Reviews of the following appeared in the Journal of Symbolic Logic 21 (1956): 381:
Popper's "Self-reference and meaning in ordinary language" (Mind 63 (1954): 162–69).
Evans's "On some semantic illusions" (Mind 63 (1954): 203–18).
Stroll's "Is everyday language inconsistent?" (Mind 63 (1954): 219–25).

_____. On some paradoxes in Analytic Philosophy, R. J. Butler, ed. (Oxford, 1962), pp. 104–19.

Toms, E. The reflexive paradoxes. Philosophical Review 61 (1952): 557–67.

_____. The liar paradox. Philosophical Review 65 (1956): 542–47.

_____. Reply to a note on the liar paradox. Philosophical Review 67 (1958): 101–05.

Tucker, J. Gödel and Epimenides. Proceedings of the Aristotelian Society 59 (1958–59): 25–48.

_____. Philosphical Arguments. Proceedings of the Aristotelian Society Supp. Vol. 39, pp. 47–64.

_____. A comment on I. J. Good's "Note on Richard's paradox" (Mind 75 (1966): 431). Mind 78 (1969): 272.

Turquette, A. R. Review of Thompson's "The logical paradoxes and Pierce's Semiotic" (Journal of Philosophy 46 (1949): 513–36). Journal of Symbolic Logic 16 (1951): 214–15.

Urbach, B. Über das Wesen der logischen Paradoxa. Zeitschrift für Philosophie und Philosophische Kritik 140 (1910): 81–108.

_____. Das Logische Paradoxon. Annalen du Philosophie und philosophische Kritik 6 (1927–28): 161–76, 265–73.

Ushenko, A. P. A modification of the theory of types. Monist 44 (1934): 147–49.

_____. A new Epimenides. Mind 46 (1937): 549–50.

_____. The Problems of Logic (London, Princeton, 1941), esp. Chap. 2.

_____. Undecidable statements and metalanguage. Mind 53 (1944): 258–62.

_____. A note on the semantic conception of truth. Philosophy and Phenomenological Research 5 (1944): 104–07.

_____. A note on the liar paradox. Mind 64 (1955): 543.

_____. An addendum to the note on the liar paradox. Mind 66 (1957): 98.

Valpola, V. Elementare Untersuchungen der Antinomien von Russell, Grelling-Nelson und Eubulides. Theoria 19 (1953): 183–88.

van Fraassen, B. C. Presupposition, implication, and self-reference. Journal of Philosophy 65 (1968): 136–52.

_____. Presuppositions, supervaluations, and free logic in The Logical Way of Doing Things, K. Lambert, ed. (New Haven, 1969).

Veatch, H. B., and Young, T. Metaphysics and the paradoxes. Review of Metaphysics 6 (1952): 199–218.

von Wright, G. H. The heterological paradox. Societas Scientarium Fennica, Commentationes physico-mathematicae, vol. 24.

_____. Review of Skolem's "De Logiske paradokser og botemidlene mot dem" (Norsk Matematisk tidskrift 32 (1950): 2–11). Journal of Symbolic Logic 16 (1951): 62.

Vredenduin, P. G. J. De Paradoxen. Algemeen Nederlands tijdschrift voor wijsbegeerte en psychologie 31 (1937–38): 191–200.

Wang, H. The irreducibility of impredicative principles. Mathematische Annalen 125 (1952): 56–66.

_____. Undecidable sentences generated by semantic paradoxes. Journal of Symbolic Logic 20 (1955): 31–42.

Wedberg, A. Review of Ushenko's The Problems of Logic (London, Princeton, 1941). Philosophical Review 52 (1943): 208–11.

_____. Review of Borel's Les Paradoxes de l'infini (Paris, 1946). Journal of Symbolic Logic 14 (1949): 53–54.

Weinberg, J. A possible solution of the heterological paradox.
Philosphical Review 46 (1937): 657-59.

Whiteley, C. H. Let Epimenides lie! Analysis 19 (1958): 23-24.

Wormell, C. P. On the paradoxes of self-reference. Mind 67
(1958): 267-71.

Yuting, S. Two semantical paradoxes. Journal of Symbolic Logic
20 (1955): 119-20.